FTCE Middle Grades Mathematics 5-9

Teacher Certification Exam

By: Sharon A Wynne, M.S.

XAMonline, INC.

Boston

To obtain permission(s) to use the material from this work for any purpose, including workshops or seminars, please submit a written request to:

XAMonline, Inc.
21 Orient Avenue
Melrose, MA 02176
Toll Free 1-800-301-4647
Email: info@xamonline.com
Web www.xamonline.com
Fax: 1-617-583-5552

Library of Congress Cataloging-in-Publication Data

Wynne, Sharon A.
FTCE Middle Grades Mathematics 5-9: Teacher Certification.
    ISBN 978-1-60787-453-9

1. Middle Grades Mathematics 5-9   2. Study Guides
3. FTCE   4. Teachers' Certification & Licensure   5. Careers

Disclaimer:
The opinions expressed in this publication are the sole works of XAMonline and were created independently from the National Education Association, Educational Testing Service (ETS), any state department of education, National Evaluation Systems (NES), or other testing affiliates.

Between the time of publication and printing, changes may occur to state specific standards, as well as testing formats and website information, that are not included in part or in whole within this product. Sample test questions developed by XAMonline reflect content comparable to real tests; however, they are not former tests. XAMonline assembles content that aligns with state standards but makes no claims nor guarantees teacher candidates a passing score. Numerical scores are determined by testing companies such as NES or ETS and are then compared with individual state standards. A passing score varies from state to state.

Printed in the United States of America   œ-1

FTCE Middle Grades Mathematics 5-9
ISBN: 978-1-60787-453-9

About the Subject Assessments

FTCE™: Subject Assessment in the Middle Grades Mathematics 5-9 Examination

Purpose: The assessments are designed to test the knowledge and competencies of prospective secondary level teachers. The question bank from which the assessments are drawn is undergoing constant revision. As a result, your test may include questions that will not count towards your score.

Test Version: There are two versions of subject assessment for mathematics examination in Florida.

The Middle Grades Mathematics 5-9 exam emphasizes comprehension in Knowledge of Mathematics through Problem Solving; Knowledge of Mathematical Representations; Knowledge of Mathematics through Reasoning; Knowledge of Mathematical Connections; Knowledge of Number Sense, Concepts, and Operations; Knowledge of Algebraic Thinking; Knowledge of Data Analysis and Probability; Knowledge of Geometry and Spatial Sense; and Knowledge of Measurement. The Middle Grades Mathematics 5-9 study guide is based on a typical knowledge level of persons who have completed a *bachelor's degree program* in mathematics.

The Mathematics 6-12 exam emphasizes comprehension in Knowledge of Algebra; Knowledge of Functions; Knowledge of Geometry from a Synthetic Perspective; Knowledge of Geometry from an Algebraic Perspective; Knowledge of Trigonometry; Knowledge of Statistics; Knowledge of Probability; Knowledge of Discrete Mathematics; Knowledge of Calculus; Knowledge of Number Sense and Mathematical Structure; Knowledge of Mathematics as Communication; Knowledge of Mathematics as Reasoning; Knowledge of Mathematical Connections; Knowledge of Instruction; and Knowledge of Assessment.

Time Allowance: You will have 2½ hours to finish the exam.

Additional Information about the FTCE Assessments: The FTCE series subject assessments are developed by the *Florida Department of Education* of Tallahassee, FL. It provides additional information on the FTCE series assessments, including registration, preparation, testing procedures, and study materials such as topical guides.

TABLE OF CONTENTS

Great Study and Testing Tips!

What to study in order to prepare for the subject assessments is the focus of this study guide but equally important is *how* you study.

You can increase your chances of truly mastering the information by taking some simple, but effective, steps.

Study Tips:

1. <u>Some foods aid the learning process</u>. Foods such as milk, nuts, seeds, rice, and oats help your study efforts by releasing natural memory enhancers called CCKs (*cholecystokinin*) composed of *tryptophan*, *choline*, and *phenylalanine*. All of these chemicals enhance the neurotransmitters associated with memory. Before studying, try a light, protein-rich meal of eggs, turkey, and fish. All of these foods release the memory enhancing chemicals. The better the connections, the more you comprehend.

Likewise, before you take a test, stick to a light snack of energy boosting and relaxing foods. A glass of milk, a piece of fruit, or some peanuts all release various memory-boosting chemicals and help you to relax and focus on the subject at hand.

2. <u>Learn to take great notes</u>. A by-product of our modern culture is that we have grown accustomed to getting our information in short doses (i.e. TV news sound bites or *USA Today* style newspaper articles.)

Consequently, we have subconsciously trained ourselves to assimilate information better in <u>neat little packages</u>. If your notes are scrawled all over the paper, it fragments the flow of the information. Strive for clarity. Newspapers use a standard format to achieve clarity. Your notes can be much clearer through use of proper formatting. A very effective format is called the *"Cornell Method."*

Take a sheet of loose-leaf lined notebook paper and draw a line all the way down the paper about 1-2" from the left-hand edge.

Draw another line across the width of the paper about 1-2" up from the bottom. Repeat this process on the reverse side of the page.

Look at the highly effective result. You have ample room for notes, a left hand margin for special emphasis items or inserting supplementary data from the textbook, a large area at the bottom for a brief summary, and a little rectangular space for just about anything you want.

3. <u>Get the concept than the details</u>. Too often, we focus on the details and do not gather an understanding of the concept. However, if you simply memorize only dates, places, or names, you may well miss the whole point of the subject.

A key way to understand things is to put them in your own words. If you are working from a textbook, automatically summarize each paragraph in your mind. If you are outlining text, do not simply copy the author's words.

Rephrase them in your own words. You remember your own thoughts and words much better than someone else has and subconsciously tend to associate the important details with the core concepts.

4. <u>Ask Why?</u> Pull apart written material paragraph by paragraph and do not forget the captions under the illustrations.

<u>Example</u>: If the heading is "Stream Erosion," flip it around to read, "Why do streams erode?" Then answer the questions.

If you train your mind to think in a series of questions and answers, not only will you learn more, but it also helps to lessen the test anxiety because you are used to answering questions.

5. <u>Read for reinforcement and future needs</u>. Even if you only have ten minutes, put your notes or a book in your hand. Your mind is similar to a computer; you have to input data in order to have it processed. *By reading, you are creating the neural connections for future retrieval.* The more times you read something, the more you reinforce the learning of ideas.

Even if you do not fully understand something on the first pass, *your mind stores much of the material for later recall.*

6. <u>Relax to learn, so go into exile</u>. Our bodies respond to an inner clock called biorhythms. Burning the midnight oil works well for some people but not everyone.

If possible, set aside a particular place to study that is free of distractions. Shut off the television, cell phone, and pager and exile your friends and family during your study period.

If you really are bothered by silence, try background music. Light classical music at a low volume has been shown over other types to aid in concentration. Music without lyrics that evokes pleasant emotions is highly suggested. Try just about anything by Mozart. It relaxes you.

7. <u>Use arrows not highlighters</u>. At best, it is difficult to read a page full of yellow, pink, blue, and green streaks. Try staring at a neon sign for a while and you will soon see that the horde of colors obscures the message.

A quick note, a brief dash of color, an underline, or an arrow pointing to a particular passage is much clearer than a horde of highlighted words.

8. <u>Budget your study time</u>. Although you should not ignore any of the material, *allocate your available study time in the same ratio that topics may appear on the test.*

Testing Tips:

1. Get smart; play dumb. Do not read anything into the question. Do not assume that the test writer is looking for something else than what is asked. Stick to the question as written and do not read extra things into it.

2.   Read the question and all the choices *twice* before answering the question. You may miss something by not carefully reading, and then re-reading, both the question and the answers.

If you really do not have a clue as to the right answer, leave it blank on the first time through. Go on to the other questions, as they may provide a clue as to how to answer the skipped questions.

If later on, you still cannot answer the skipped ones . . . *Guess.* The only penalty for guessing is that you *might* get it wrong. Only one thing is certain; if you do not put anything down, you will get it wrong!

3. Turn the question into a statement. Look at the way the questions are worded. The syntax of the question usually provides a clue. Does it seem more familiar as a statement rather than as a question? Does it sound strange?

By turning a question into a statement, you may be able to spot if an answer sounds right, and it may trigger memories of material you have read.

4. Look for hidden clues. It is actually very difficult to compose multiple-foil (choice) questions without giving away part of the answer in the options presented.

In most multiple-choice questions, you can often readily eliminate one or two of the potential answers. This leaves you with only two real possibilities and automatically your odds go to fifty-fifty for very little work.

5. Trust your instincts. For every fact that you have read, you subconsciously retain something of that knowledge. On questions that you are not certain about, go with your basic instincts. **Your first impression on how to answer a question is usually correct.**

6. Mark your answers directly on the test booklet. Do not bother trying to fill in the optical scan sheet on the first pass through the test.

Just be very careful not to mis-mark your answers when you eventually transcribe them to the scan sheet.

7. Watch the clock! You have a set amount of time to answer the questions. Do not get bogged down trying to answer a single question at the expense of ten questions you can more readily answer.

COMPETENCY 1   **KNOWLEDGE OF MATHEMATICS THROUGH PROBLEM SOLVING**

Skill 1.1   Identify appropriate mathematical problems from real-world situations.

Numbers are everywhere, at the gas station, in the weather forecast, in the ups and downs of the stock market. Shopping is the most common real-world situation in which mathematical skills are needed. Following are several examples of the application of mathematics to this everyday activity.

The unit rate for purchasing an item is its price divided by the number of ounces, pounds, and gallons, etc. of the item. The item with the lower unit rate has the lower price.

Example: Lorna went to a Deli looking for the best deal to buy homemade chili. These are the prices she found:

$1.79 for 10 ounces
$1.89 for 12 ounces
$5.49 for 32 ounces

Find the item with the lowest unit price (price per ounce):

$$\frac{\$1.79}{10oz.} = \$0.179/oz \qquad \frac{\$1.89}{12oz.} = \$0.1575/oz. \qquad \frac{\$5.49}{32oz.} = \$0.172/oz.$$

$1.89 for 12 ounces is the best price.

Unit prices can also be calculated by setting up proportions (see Skill 5.10).

Example: Andrew went to two different stores to buy a special kind of bolt. In Store 1, he found a box containing 40 bolts for $8.19. In Store 2, he found a box containing 22 bolts for $4.89. Which store has the best deal?

Using a proportion to find the price per bolt at each store:

Store 1

$$\frac{40\ bolts}{\$8.19} = \frac{1\ bolt}{\$x}$$

$$40x = 8.19$$
$$x = \$0.2048$$

Store 2

$$\frac{22 \; bolts}{\$4.89} = \frac{1 \; bolt}{\$x}$$

$$22x = 4.89$$
$$x = \$0.2223$$

Since $\$0.2048 < \$0.2223$, Store 1 has the better deal.

Another way to apply mathematical problems to real-life situations is when calculating taxes and price after taxes. To find the amount of sales tax on an item, change the percent of sales tax into an equivalent decimal number by moving the decimal point two places to the left. Then multiply the decimal number by the price of the object to find the sales tax. The total cost of an item will be the price of the item plus the sales tax.

Example: A guitar costs $120 plus 7% sales tax. How much are the sales tax and the total bill?

7% = 0.07 in decimal form
(0.07)($120) = $8.40 sales tax
$120 + $8.40 = $128.40 ← total cost

An alternative method to find the total cost is to multiply the price times the factor 1.07 (price + sales tax):

$$\$120 \times 1.07 = \$128.40$$

This gives you the total cost in fewer steps.

Example: A suit costs $450 plus 6.5% sales tax. How much are the sales tax and the total bill?

6.5% = 0.065 in decimal form
(0.065)(450) = $29.25 sales tax
$450 + $29.25 = $479.25 total cost

Using the alternative method to find total cost, multiply the price times the factor 1.065 (price + sales tax):

$$\$450.00 \times 1.065 = \$479.25$$

This gives you the total cost in fewer steps.

Another kind of real-world mathematical calculation involves time. Elapsed time problems are usually one of two types. One type of problem is the elapsed time between two times given in hours, minutes and seconds. The other common type of problem is between two times given in months and years.

For any time of day past noon, change to military time by adding 12 hours. For instance, 1:15 p.m. would be 13:15. Remember when you borrow a minute or an hour in a subtraction problem that you have borrowed 60 more seconds or minutes.

Example: Sharon was given the order to transport a truck of supplies from her base to an airport in less than 4 hours. She departed the base exactly at 11:34:22 a.m. and arrived at her destination at 3:28:40 p.m. Did Sharon fulfill her mission on time?

Convert 3:28:40 p.m. to military time

$$
\begin{array}{r}
3{:}28{:}40 \\
+\ 12{:}00{:}00 \\
\hline
15{:}28{:}40
\end{array}
$$

Now subtract

$$
\begin{array}{r}
15{:}28{:}40 \\
-\ 11{:}34{:}22 \\
\hline
{:}18
\end{array}
$$

Borrow an hour and add 60 more minutes. Subtract.

$$
\begin{array}{r}
14{:}88{:}40 \\
-\ 11{:}34{:}22 \\
\hline
3{:}54{:}18
\end{array}
$$
↔ 3 hours, 54 minutes, 18 seconds

Yes, Sharon fulfilled her mission on time.

Example: John lived in Arizona from September 1991 until March 1995. How long is that?

		Year	Month
March 1995	=	95	03
September 1991	= −	91	09

Borrow a year and convert it into 12 more months, **subtract**.

	Year	Month
March 1995	94	15
September 1991	− 91	09
	3 yrs	6 months

Example: A race took the winner 1 hr. 58 min. 12 sec. on the first half of the race and 2 hr. 9 min. 57 sec. on the second half of the race. How much time did the entire race take?

```
  1 hr.  58 min.  12 sec.
+ 2 hr.   9 min.  57 sec.      [Add]
  3 hr.  67 min.  69 sec.
          + 1 min. –60 sec.    [Convert 60 sec. to 1 min.]
  3 hr.  68 min.   9 sec.
+ 1 hr.–60 min.               [Convert 60 min. to 1 hr.]
  4 hr.   8 min.   9 sec.   ← Final answer
```

For more examples, see **Essential Tips for Every Math Teacher** (section **Real life examples**) at the end of this guide.

Skill 1.2   Apply problem-solving strategies to solve non-routine problems with multiple steps.

Teachers can promote problem solving by allowing multiple attempts at problems. Teachers should be familiar with several specific problem-solving skills.

The **guess-and-check** strategy calls for students to make an initial guess at the solution, check the answer, and use the outcome of to guide the next guess. With each successive guess, the student should get closer to the correct answer. Constructing a table from the guesses can help organize the data.

Example: There are 100 coins in a jar. Ten are dimes. The rest are pennies and nickels. There are twice as many pennies as nickels. How many pennies and nickels are in the jar?

There are 90 total nickels and pennies in the jar (100 coins – 10 dimes).

There are twice as many pennies as nickels. Make guesses that fulfill the criteria and adjust based on the answer found. Continue until we find the correct answer, 60 pennies and 30 nickels.

Number of Pennies	Number of Nickels	Total Number of Pennies and Nickels
40	20	60
80	40	120
70	35	105
60	30	90

When solving a problem where the final result and the steps to reach the result are given, students must **work backwards** to determine what the starting point must have been.

Example: John subtracted 7 from his age and divided the difference by 3. The result was 4. What is John's age?

> Work backward by reversing the operations.
> $4 \times 3 = 12$
> $12 + 7 = 19$
> John is 19 years old.

For more ideas about problem solving see **Essential Tips for Every Math Teacher** (in particular the section **Word problem strategies**) at the end of this guide.

Skill 1.3   Evaluate the reasonableness of results from the original problem.

Estimation and approximation may be used to check the reasonableness of answers (See Skill 5.2). Students should also re-read the original problem after arriving at a solution and assess whether the solution makes sense.

Skill 1.4   Apply appropriate mathematical concepts and procedures to solve problems in various contexts.

Artists, musicians, scientists, social scientists, and business people use mathematical modeling to solve problems in their disciplines. These disciplines rely on the tools and symbols of mathematics to model natural events and manipulate data. Mathematics is a key aspect of visual art.

Artists use the geometric properties of shapes, ratios, and proportions in creating paintings and sculptures. For example, mathematics is essential to the concept of perspective. Artists must determine the appropriate lengths and heights of objects to portray three-dimensional distance in two dimensions.

Mathematics is also an important part of music. Many musical terms have mathematical connections. For example, the musical octave contains twelve notes and spans a factor of two in frequency. In other words, the frequency, the speed of vibration that determines tone and sound quality, doubles from the first note in an octave to the last. Thus, starting from any note we can determine the frequency of any other note with the following formula.

$$\text{Freq} = \text{note} \times 2^{N/12}$$

Where N is the number of notes from the starting point and note is the frequency of the starting note. Mathematical understanding of frequency plays an important role in the tuning of musical instruments.

In addition to the visual and auditory arts, mathematics is an integral part of most scientific disciplines. The uses of mathematics in science are almost endless. The following are but a few examples of how scientists use mathematics. Physical scientists use vectors, functions, derivatives, and integrals to describe and model the movement of objects. Biologists and ecologists use mathematics to model ecosystems and study DNA. Finally, chemists use mathematics to study the interaction of molecules and to determine proper amounts and proportions of reactants.

Many social science disciplines use mathematics to model and solve problems. Economists, for example, use functions, graphs, and matrices to model the activities of producers, consumers, and firms. Political scientists use mathematics to model the behavior and opinions of the electorate. Finally, sociologists use mathematical functions to model the behavior of humans and human populations.

Finally, mathematical problem solving and modeling is essential to business planning and execution. For example, businesses rely on mathematical projections to plan business strategy. Additionally, stock market analysis and accounting rely on mathematical concepts.

Skill 1.5   Evaluate the validity of mathematical arguments (e.g., a justification that the sum of two odd numbers is always even)

One critical skill in mathematics is identification of valid mathematical arguments. **A valid argument, generally, is an argument in which the conclusion necessarily follows from the premises.** If the argument is valid and the premises are true, then the argument is sound. Thus, valid mathematical arguments are deductive in nature.

The first step to determining whether a mathematical argument is valid, then, is to **identify the premises**. These premises may or may not be explicit in the argument; in some cases, the premises may be unmentioned mathematical theorems or axioms (such as the Pythagorean Theorem, for instance). The need for (or use of) particular premises in a given argument may become apparent only after starting the analysis of the argument or proof under consideration.

After identifying the premises or axioms associated with the argument, the next step is to **evaluate the proof of the conclusion** of the argument. **A valid mathematical proof requires demonstration of the truth of the conclusion for all possible cases**. It is not sufficient to simply show that the conclusion is valid in certain cases and then, reasoning by induction, conclude that the argument is true. Such inductive reasoning, although appropriate in some other contexts, is a weaker form of reasoning that does not constitute a valid mathematical argument. On the other hand, **disproving a particular conclusion requires only a single counterexample**. Therefore, simply showing one case where the conclusion of the argument is false (when all the premises are true) is sufficient to demonstrate that the argument is not valid.

Consider the conclusion of an example argument, "The sum of two odd numbers is always even." The argument might include the following reasoning.

"An even number is divisible by two, but an odd number is not (dividing an odd number by two leaves a remainder of magnitude one). Define positive integers m and n each as some odd number. Then:

$$\frac{m}{2} = a + \frac{1}{2} \quad \text{and} \quad \frac{n}{2} = b + \frac{1}{2}$$

In this case, a and b are both positive integers, and the remainder from the division becomes the added term of $\frac{1}{2}$. Next, add m and n and divide by two:

$$\frac{m+n}{2} = \frac{m}{2} + \frac{n}{2} = \left(a + \frac{1}{2}\right) + \left(b + \frac{1}{2}\right) = a + b + 1$$

The result of dividing the sum of m and n by two is $a + b + 1$; this is an integer value. As a result, the sum of m and n is divisible by two. The same reasoning works for negative odd numbers (simply subtract $\frac{1}{2}$ instead of adding $\frac{1}{2}$ in the above expressions) or with one negative odd number and one positive odd number, so the sum of two odd numbers is even."

By following the reasoning of the argument and showing that each step is legitimate, it is possible to demonstrate that the argument is valid. In this case, because the premises of the argument are true, the argument is both valid and sound. The argument may be presented in a less formal, conversational style, as with the above example, or it may be presented in a more formal, point-by-point style that clearly lists each step (and its justification) for the proof.

Another example might entail, for instance, an argument that the sum of any three consecutive natural numbers is divisible by 6. To demonstrate that this is not a true statement, it is sufficient to find a counterexample. Try several cases:

$$1 + 2 + 3 = 6$$
$$2 + 3 + 4 = 9$$

In the first case, the result is 6, which is divisible by 6. In the second case, however, the result is 9. The number 9 is not divisible by 6, so a counterexample has been found, and the statement has been shown to be false.

In some instances, the conclusion of the argument may be true, but it does not follow from the premises. In such an instance, the argument must be demonstrated to be invalid by showing that the conclusion does not follow from the premises. For instance, consider an argument that attempts to show that the sum of any three consecutive natural numbers is divisible by 3. It is indeed true that this is the case, but an argument for this conclusion may not be valid. Consider the argument posed in the following manner:

Premise: The sum of any three consecutive natural numbers is 8.
Conclusion: The sum of any three consecutive natural numbers is divisible by 3.

Obviously, 8 is not divisible by 3, so the conclusion (although true) cannot follow from the premises. The argument is therefore invalid.

In like manner, an unsound argument may have a true conclusion that follows from the premises, but certain premises are incorrect. Consider the above argument, slightly altered:

Premise: The sum of any three consecutive natural numbers is 6.
Conclusion: The sum of any three consecutive natural numbers is divisible by 3.

If the premise were true, then the conclusion would follow, since 6 is divisible by 3. This argument is therefore valid. Nevertheless, because the premise is false, the argument is not sound. Different arguments therefore require different methods of analysis to determine their validity. The general approach, however, is largely the same for evaluating the validity of the argument.

Skill 1.6   Predict logical conclusions from given statements

Conditional statements can be diagrammed using a **Venn diagram**. A diagram can be drawn with one circle inside another circle. The inner circle represents the hypothesis. The outer circle represents the conclusion. If the hypothesis is taken to be true, then you are located inside the inner circle. If you are located in the inner circle then you are also inside the outer circle, so that proves the conclusion is true. Sometimes that conclusion can then be used as the hypothesis for another conditional statement resulting in a second conclusion.

Example: If you are in Pittsburgh, then you are in Pennsylvania.

In this statement, "you are in Pittsburgh" is the hypothesis.
In this statement, "you are in Pennsylvania" is the conclusion.

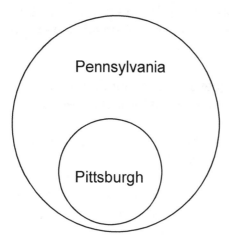

Example: Given the following statements draw a conclusion.

All swimmers are athletes.
All athletes are scholars.

In "if-then" form, these would be:

If you are a swimmer, then you are an athlete.
If you are an athlete, then you are a scholar.

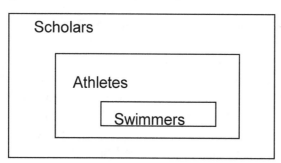

Clearly, if you are a swimmer, then you are also an athlete. This includes you in the group of scholars.

Example: Given the following statements draw a conclusion.

All swimmers are athletes.
All wrestlers are athletes.

In "if-then" form, these would be:

If you are a swimmer, then you are an athlete.
If you are a wrestler, then you are an athlete.

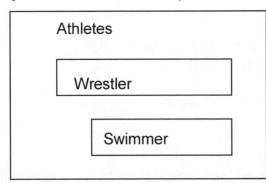

Clearly, if you are a swimmer or a wrestler, then you are also an athlete. This does not allow you to come to any other conclusions.

A swimmer may or may not also be a wrestler. Therefore, no conclusion is possible.

Example: Given the following statements, draw a conclusion.

All rectangles are parallelograms.
Quadrilateral ABCD is not a parallelogram.

In "if-then" form, the first statement would be:
If a figure is a rectangle, then it is also a parallelogram.

Note that the second statement is the negation of the conclusion of statement one. Remember also that the contrapositive is logically equivalent to a given conditional. That is, **"If q, then p"**. Since "ABCD is **not** a parallelogram" is saying **"If q,"** then you can come to the conclusion **"then p."** Therefore, the conclusion is ABCD is not a rectangle. Looking at the Venn diagram below, if all rectangles are parallelograms, then rectangles are included as part of the parallelograms. Since quadrilateral ABCD is not a parallelogram, it is excluded from anywhere inside the parallelogram box. This allows you to conclude that ABCD cannot be a rectangle either.

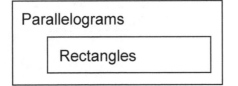

quadrilateral
ABCD

Try These. *(The answers are in the Answer Key to Practice Problems)*:

What conclusion, if any, can be reached? Assume each statement is true, regardless of any personal beliefs.

1. If the Red Sox make it to the World Series, I will buy World Series tickets.
   I bought World Series tickets.

2. If an angle's measure is between 0° and 90°, then the angle is acute.
   Angle B is not acute.

3. Students who do well in geometry will succeed in college.
   Annie is doing extremely well in geometry.

4. Left-handed people are witty and charming.
   You are left-handed.

Skill 1.7 Identify appropriate instructional strategies to facilitate student understanding of problem solving

Instructional strategies are content-specific-information based strategies through the literacy skills of reading, writing, listening, viewing and presenting that allow students to acquire and retain content knowledge and content-specific abilities.(SDE.ct.gov)

The instructional strategies provided in this section are only part of a vast array of effective strategies teachers may use to present, teach and assess real-life situations that call for mathematical calculation.

DRTA –Directed Reading-Thinking Activity is a comprehension strategy in the form of a discussion format that includes students using their background knowledge to make predictions and then evaluate their solutions.

Example: Gary has two black balls, five white balls and three orange balls inside a bag. If Gary takes a ball from the bag ten times replacing it each time, make a prediction of how many of each ball he will get. Then, compare it to the actual results Gary obtained and explain why they are the same or different.

Your predictions	Gary's results
	Orange: 2 times Black: 1 time White: 7 times

The prediction should follow the laws of probabilities:

$$P_{white} = \frac{5}{2+3+5} = \frac{5}{10} = \frac{1}{2}$$

$$P_{black} = \frac{2}{2+3+5} = \frac{2}{10} = \frac{1}{5}$$

$$P_{orange} = \frac{3}{2+3+5} = \frac{3}{10}$$

To calculate the most probable outcome, we multiply the probability of each color to be selected by the amount of attempts.

$$Orange = P_{orange} \times 10 = 3 \, times$$

$$White = P_{white} \times 10 = (1/2)10 = 5 \, times$$

$$Black = P_{black} \times 10 = (1/5)10 = 2 \, times$$

Your prediction	Gary's results
Orange: 3 times	Orange: 2 times
Black: 2 times	Black: 1 time
White: 5 times	White: 7 times

The outcomes were not the same because the calculated values represent the most probable outcome, not the only possible outcome of the event. If Gary keeps doing the same experiment repeatedly, the majority of the results he will get will coincide with the predictions.

QAR –Question–Answer Relationship strategy targets the question "Where is the answer?" inside a given problem. We have three types of activities in which the answers must be

1. A "right there" type of activity where the answer is somewhere in the stem and body of the question (multiple choice type of question with Depth of Knowledge (DOK) 1),
2. Students must "think and search" by putting information together and making inferences (DOK 2); and
3. An "on your own" type of activity for which the answer must come from the students' background knowledge (open-ended DOK 3 type).

Example "right there":
Maria is 12 years old. Mario's age is 9 years more than one-third Maria's age, and Martha is one year older than Mario. How is old is the youngest of the three?

Mario's age is the one we need to find.

Mario $= 12 \div 3 + 9 = 13$ years old. Maria is 12 and Martha is 14 years old. So, Maria is the youngest of the three.

Example "think and search":
A farmer has 15 cows inside a pen like the one below.

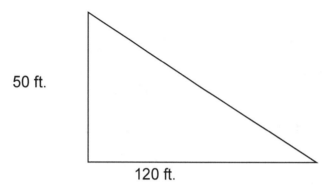

50 ft.

120 ft.

How many square feet are available for each cow in the pen?

First, we write the expression to calculate the square feet per cow:

$$A_{cow} = A_{pen} \div \#_{cows} = A_{pen} \div 15$$

The area of the pen is the area of a right triangle.
$A_{triangle}$ = (½) base x height = (½)120ft. x 50 ft. = 3,000 ft^2
Then, A_{cow} = 3,000 ft^2 ÷15 = 200 ft^2 per cow.

Example "on your own":
If an inspector visited the farmer's facilities and told him that the norm was 250 square foot per cow. How would the lengths of either known dimension of the pen need to be changed to achieve the norm?

Prediction: enlarge one of the sides of the pen /triangle.
If A_{cow} = 250 ft^2, the pen should have an area of at least 3750 ft^2.

So, calculate how to change either side by keeping one of the sides the same while changing the other. If the 50 ft side is kept:

A_{pen} = (½) base x height = (½) base x 50 ft. = 3750 ft^2.

Solve for the base and find base = 150 ft. Therefore, the base of the pen should be 150 feet long.

Comparison Matrix: the teacher writes the subjects, categories and topics across the top of the matrix (aka box or table) and writes the facts, details, attributes, characteristics, features etc., down the left column of the chart. Then the student needs to complete the matrix.

Example: Mario has three shapes in his hands and no measuring tools. Use the interior angle expression to help Mario complete the following chart.

Complete the matrix:

name	# of sides	Interior angles	Number of vertices
square	4	90	4
pentagon	5	108	5
hexagon	6	120	6
n-gon	n	$180° - (360° \div n)$	n

We get every answer by substituting 4, 5 and 6 in the expression $180° - (360° \div n)$

Classification Chart is a similar strategy to the Comparison Matrix, only this chart does not include the facts, details, attributes, characteristics, features etc. In the left column and there should be a specific reason students need to recognize the similarities between the provided topics and details.

Example: Susan has five chickens. The following are the weights of those chickens {4, 4, 6, 7, 9}.

Complete the table below with the definition and the values of the mean, median, mode and range.

mean	median	mode	range
Average of a set of numbers	Middle number in a sorted list of numbers	Number which appears the most in a set of numbers	The difference between the lowest and highest values of a set of numbers
$(4 + 4 + 6 + 7 + 9) \div 5$ $= 30 \div 5 = 6$	6	4	5

What is the median if Susan buys another 9-pound chicken?

{4, 4, 6, 7, 9, 9} is an even set of numbers. Therefore, we take the two central values and obtain the median: $(6 + 7) \div 2 = 6.5$

Visualizing is a very useful strategy when solving problems because the best way to make sense of some mathematical problems is to create an image of them. Visualization skills include internalizing, identifying, comparing, connecting and sharing. We use visualizing strategies to step into a problem, to model the problem and to formulate a plan. We can use visualization to step into a problem.

Example: Imagine that you have a stack of ten cards in numerical order with 1 at the top, down to 10 at the bottom. Move three cards in sets of three from the top to the bottom and look at the card at the bottom of the deck each time. Repeat this 7 times.

Write the list that results from this operation.

In this case, the first three moves are easy to predict: 3, 6, 9. The next four numbers will be 2, 5, 8, 1. So, the list is: {3, 6, 9, 2, 5, 8, 1}.

We can also use visualization to model a problem when the situation described is physically unattainable.

Example: Manny has interlocking cubes. One red cube, fifty green cubes and 200 blue cubes. If Manny wants to cover the yellow cube completely with green cubes and cover the resulting cube completely with blue cubes, how many green and blue cubes will Manny need?

We can help model the situation by making the yellow cube a 1x1x1 cube inside the volume of 3^3(1x1x1 cubes).

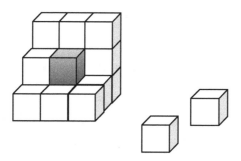

So, we can easily see that the total amount of green cubes needed is $3^3-1=26$. We can do the same with the resulting green cube and the amount of blue cubes needed to completely cover it: $5^3-3^3=98$ blue cubes. The model helps us see this was a problem of volumes.

You can also use visualization to plan or resolve a problem by inferring a solution. You cannot answer a guessing type of question without visualizing.

Example: Alfred wants to buy flower arrangements for every room in his motel. Each flower arrangement costs $30, and he wants to spend no more than $1200. If the motel has 47 rooms, what percentage of the rooms will still need flower arrangements?

You visualize each time the "if" question is asked.

$$\$30 \cdot x \leq \$1200$$
$$x \leq 40$$

where x is the number of flower arrangements.

Since there are 47 rooms, 7 will not have flower arrangements. To find the percentage that still need flower arrangements:

$$\frac{7}{p} = \frac{47}{100} \rightarrow p = 14.89\%$$

14.89% of the rooms will still need flower arrangements.

These are examples are easy problems, but we can use this strategy to answer very intricate problems too.

Graphic Organizers –Graphic organizers are visual representations of ideas and information. They often provide a useful way for students to organize and clarify information, and can guide a student's thinking as they build on a starting visual map or diagram. Venn diagrams, box-and-whisker diagrams and tree diagrams are but a few examples. Students should be familiar with and be able to use a variety of graphic organizers.

Example: One vendor sold items in the School Fair. The list below represents the price in dollars of the items sold.

99, 8, 9, 5, 14, 25, 88, 76, 74, 60, 62, 62, 73, 55, 45, 49, 17, 33, 26

Draw a histogram using the proper intervals for this data set. Explain why you choose the intervals you used. Then use your diagram to say how many more items over $60 were sold than the items for less than $40. Explain your answer. In this case, it is obvious that the selection of the interval is key to producing a correct histogram.

The data set distribution calls for a $20 interval because that sets a reasonable number of horizontal bars and no bar has too many items in it. So, then we use the histogram to solve the second part of the question.

School Fair Sales

The total amount of items sold under $40 is 8 and over $60 are 8, so, the answer is 8–8=0. The amount of items sold in less than $40 is the same than the number of items sold over $60.

Example: Mercedes has two pairs of shoes, one black and one brown, two shirts, one pink and one white and two pants, one black and one blue. In how many ways can Mercedes dress herself to go to school?

A tree diagram is the best fit for the situation. By developing the diagram, the student is visually modeling the problem, as well solving it by laying out all possible combinations.

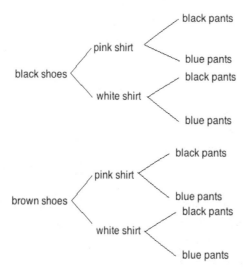

So, Mercedes can dress in 8 different ways.

Skill 1.8   Distinguish between deductive and inductive reasoning in a given situation

Inductive thinking is the process of finding a pattern from a group of examples. The pattern is then used to draw, predict or support a conclusion. The conclusion may or may not be true because other examples may not follow the predicted pattern.

Deductive thinking is the process of arriving at a conclusion based on other statements that are all known to be true, such as theorems, axioms, or postulates. Conclusions found by deductive thinking based on true statements will **always** be true.

A postulate is an accepted property of real numbers or geometric figures that cannot be proven.

Example:
On Monday, Mr. Peterson eats breakfast at a diner.
On Tuesday, Mr. Peterson eats breakfast at the same diner.
On Wednesday, Mr. Peterson eats breakfast the diner again.
On Thursday, Mr. Peterson eats breakfast at the diner again.

Conclusion: On Friday, Mr. Peterson will eat breakfast at the diner again. This is a conclusion based on inductive reasoning. Based on several days' observations, you conclude that Mr. Peterson will eat at a diner. This may or may not be true, but it is a conclusion based on inductive thinking.

Example: The following algebraic postulates are frequently used as reasons for statements in two column geometric proofs:

Addition Property: If $a = b$ and $c = d$, then $a + c = b + d$.

Subtraction Property: If a = b and c = d, then a - c = b - d.

Multiplication Property: If $a = b$ and $c \neq 0$, then $ac = bc$.

Division Property: If $a = b$ and $c \neq 0$, then $a/c = b/c$.

Reflexive Property:	$a = a$
Symmetric Property:	If $a = b$, then $b = a$.
Transitive Property:	If $a = b$ and $b = c$, then $a = c$.
Distributive Property:	$a(b + c) = ab + ac$
Substitution Property:	If $a = b$, then b may be substituted for a in any other expression (a may also be substituted for b).

In a two column proof, the left side of the proof should be the given information, or statements that could be proved by deductive reasoning. The right column of the proof consists of the reasons used to determine that each statement to the left was verifiably true. The right side can identify given information, or state theorems, postulates, definitions, or algebraic properties used to prove that particular line of the proof is true.

To write indirect proofs, assume the opposite of the conclusion. Keep your hypothesis and given information the same. Proceed to develop the steps of the proof, looking for a statement that contradicts your original assumption or some other known fact. This contradiction indicates that the assumption you made at the beginning of the proof was incorrect; therefore, the original conclusion has to be true.

Simple example of an indirect proof (using a paragraph proof):

Given: $3x + 5 = 17$
Prove: $x \neq 3$

Assume the opposite of the conclusion and proceed until a contradiction is reached. In this example, assume $x = 3$. If this is true, then $3(3) + 5 = 17$. Substituting into the given, $3(3) + 5 = 9 + 5 \neq 17$. So $x \neq 3$.

Simple example of a direct proof (using a two column proof):

Given: $3x + 5 = 17$
Prove: $x = 4$

Statement	Reason
$3x + 5 = 17$	Given
$3x = 12$	Subtraction property of equality
$x = 4$	Division property of equality

**COMPETENCY 2   KNOWLEDGE OF MATHEMATICAL
MANIPULATIVES AND MODELS**

**Skill 2.1   Identify appropriate representations or models for
mathematics operations or situations using written, concrete,
pictorial, graphical, or algebraic methods**

According to Piaget, there are four primary cognitive structures or development stages: sensorimotor, pre-operations, concrete operations, and formal operations. In the sensorimotor stage (0-2 years), intelligence takes the form of motor actions. In the pre-operation stage (3-7 years), intelligence is intuitive in nature. Intelligence in the concrete operational stage (8-11 years) is logical but depends upon concrete referents. In the final stage of formal operations (12-15 years), thinking involves abstractions.

Even though middle school students are typically ready to approach mathematics in abstract ways, some of them still require concrete referents such as manipulatives and visual aids. It is useful to keep in mind that the developmental stages of individuals vary. In addition, different people have different learning styles, some tending more towards the visual and others relatively verbal. Research has shown that learning is most effective when information is presented through multiple modalities or representations. Most mathematics textbooks now use this multi-modal approach.

Throughout this guide, mathematical operations and situations are represented through words, both verbally and written, algebraic symbols, geometric diagrams (e.g. pictures & illustrations, etc.), and graphs. A few commonly used representations are discussed below.

The basic mathematical operations include addition, subtraction, multiplication and division. In word problems, these are represented by the following typical expressions:

Addition can be indicated by: sum, greater than and more than, increased by and added to.

Subtraction can be expressed by: difference, fewer than, minus, less than, decreased by, and subtracted from.

Multiplication is shown by: product, times, multiplied by and twice.

Division is used for: quotient, divided by and ratio.

<u>Example</u>: Verbal and symbolic representations of basic mathematical operations:

Nancy had *n* apples and she bought 7 more:
(7 added to a number) $n + 7$

Nancy had *n* apples and she gave away 8:
(a number decreased by 8) $n - 8$

Nancy now has 12 times the apples she had at the beginning and she shares them equally between seven of her friends:
(12 times a number divided by 7) $12n \div 7$

Nancy had *n* apples and she gave away 28:
(28 less than a number) $n - 28$

The amount of apples Nancy has is to 55:
(the ratio of a number to 55) $n/55$

Nancy bought four times the sum of 21 plus the amount of apples she had:
(4 times the sum of a number and 21) $4(n + 21)$

Mathematical operations can be shown using manipulatives or drawings.

Multiplication can be shown using an array of different manipulatives.

   3×4 may be expressed as 3 rows of 4 each

☐ ☐ ☐ ☐
☐ ☐ ☐ ☐
☐ ☐ ☐ ☐

Addition and subtractions can be demonstrated with symbols.
   ψ ψ ψ ξ ξ ξ ξ
   $3 + 4 = 7$
   $7 - 3 = 4$

Fractions can be represented using pattern blocks, fraction bars, or paper folding.

Example:

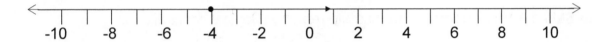

$\frac{1}{8}$		$\frac{1}{8}$		$\frac{1}{8}$		$\frac{1}{8}$		$\frac{1}{8}$		$\frac{1}{8}$		$\frac{1}{8}$		$\frac{1}{8}$	
$\frac{1}{4}$				$\frac{1}{4}$				$\frac{1}{4}$				$\frac{1}{4}$			
$\frac{1}{2}$								$\frac{1}{2}$							

Diagrams of arithmetic operations can present mathematical data in visual form. For example, a number line can be used to add and subtract.

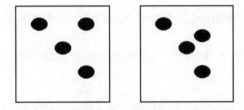

Five added to negative four on the number line or $-4 + 5 = 1$.

Pictorial representations can also be used to explain the arithmetic processes.

Two groups of four equal eight or $2 \times 4 = 8$ shown in picture form.

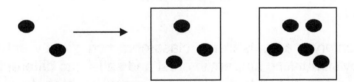

Adding two objects to three or $2 + 3 = 5$ shown in picture form.

Many more examples of different kinds of mathematical representations can be found in the following sections.

Skill 2.2 Interpret results as illustrated by the use of mathematical representations.

Mathematical results can be represented numerically, pictorially or graphically and often through technology for ease of interpretation. Diagrams or graphs present the results as a whole and allow one to take in the entire situation at a glance. A middle school student should be able to select and include the appropriate technology for learning, interpreting and modeling mathematical concepts and skills. The use of technology has an additional impact on students: it motivates them to learn. It makes them free to learn actively. Activities that were considered dull with traditional means like paper and pen can now be resolved in a more creative way. Interactive interpretation with multiple representations allow students to explore abstract concepts in many different ways at a time, enhancing the success of both verbal and visual learners; promoting a deeper understanding and better, more polished answers, since the computer environment supports easy editions and corrections.

The following are some of the sections in this guide that deal with the interpretation of mathematical results:

In **Skill 1.6** Venn diagrams are used to represent logical conclusions.

In **Skill 2.3** technology is used to teach and interpret mathematical concepts.

Skills 6.2 and **6.7** show the relationships between two variables represented using graphs.

Skills 6.6 and **8.3** show real world relationships of data in graphical format

Skills 8.2 and **8.3** deals with data sets and their graphical representations.

| Skill 2.3 | Select appropriate manipulatives, mathematical models, or technology for teaching particular mathematics concepts (e.g., tiles for teaching area, graphing calculators for teaching algebra) |

The use of supplementary materials in the classroom can greatly enhance the learning experience by stimulating student interest and satisfying different learning styles. Manipulatives, models, and technology are examples of tools available to teachers.

Manipulatives are materials that students can physically handle and move. Manipulatives allow students to understand mathematic concepts by allowing them to see concrete examples of abstract processes. Manipulatives are attractive to students because they appeal to the students' visual and tactile senses. Available for all levels of math, manipulatives are useful tools for reinforcing operations and concepts. They are not, however, a substitute for the development of sound computational skills.

Models are another means of representing mathematical concepts by relating the concepts to real-world situations. Teachers must choose wisely when devising and selecting models because, to be effective, models must be applied properly. For example, a building with floors above and below ground is a good model for introducing the concept of negative numbers. It would be difficult, however, to use the building model in teaching subtraction of negative numbers.

Finally, there are many forms of **technology** available to math teachers. For example, students can test their understanding of math concepts by working on skill specific computer programs and websites. Graphing calculators can help students visualize the graphs of functions. Teachers can also enhance their lectures and classroom presentations by creating multimedia presentations. Smartboards are an incredibly versatile tool, common in modern classrooms.

Technology is increasingly important in schools today. Knowing what each item is, how to use each item and the importance of each item beyond the walls of the school is extremely important for teachers and students. Technology tools change rapidly. Teachers should make every effort to keep pace and use available tools to enhance students' learning.

While computers and other technology devices cannot replace teachers, they can be used to enhance the curriculum. Computers, for example, may be used to help students practice basic skills. Many excellent programs exist to encourage higher-order thinking skills, creativity and problem solving. Learning to use technology appropriately is an important preparation for adulthood. Computers can also show the connections between mathematics and the real world.

See **Essential Tips for Every Math Teacher** at the end of this guide for ideas about using manipulatives, software, and other educational aids.

Skill 2.4 Use appropriate manipulatives and technology for teaching diverse groups of students (e.g., varied learning styles and exceptionalities)

America's public school system was founded upon the premise that all people, regardless of their culture or special circumstances, are entitled to a free, quality education so that they can become productive, contributing citizens in our society. To be able to achieve that, teachers need to be sensitive to their student's cultural and academic differences.

The modern classroom must celebrate diversity and use manipulatives and technology to support different teaching techniques directed to inclusion instead of mainstreaming.

Manipulatives for teaching diverse groups Teachers use different instruction by modifying the instructional delivery. One of the most important ways to aid children with special needs is to provide manipulatives that are culturally and specifically suited for them (e.g. bigger or suitable geometric shapes for children that have an

IEP, classroom money for transient students, or more complex sets for gifted students that need to be challenge beyond the curriculum.)

It is essential to be sensitive to external stimuli (hearing, sight), physical space (mobility) and general layout of the classroom. Teachers need to be able to see their classroom environment from a number of perspectives. Your own classroom is a manipulative.

Example: If you have a visually impaired student in your class and you are teaching properties of triangles in a geometry class, how would you include the visually impaired (VI) student without interrupting or delaying the learning process of the rest of the class? Take into account how the student would feel if he/she were aware of receiving special treatment. In a case like this, the use of appropriate manipulatives is desirable, not only for the VI student, but also for the rest of the class. You might also change your teaching strategy and include the use of tactile methods of shape recognition. For example, say, "Now, close your eyes and tell the shape with your hands, touch the sides of the shape and feel how many different sides it has. How many sides does this particular shape have? Are they all equal? Feel the corners, how many corners are there? Are all the corners the same?" etc....

Technology for teaching diverse groups of students: Using technology fosters belonging and interactive participation in general education classrooms for students with learning disorders (LD) (Bryant & Bryant, 1998). Mathematical concepts may be illuminated by using simple things such as pictures and graphs, or more complex resources like interactive math tools. These tools are created to help the student understand, not memorize. Teachers will need to adapt their learning strategies to the technological resources they have at hand, always keeping in mind that the best teaching tools are based on real experiences: a combination of technology and instructional strategies.

Another example of lesson modification is the use of assistive technology (AT) in the classroom and the use of specialized equipment like computers, DVD printer enlargers, DVD players, Braille material, big books, voice activated software, closed circuit monitors, TTY telephones, motorized wheelchairs, etc... These devices help all students to learn and interact at the best level possible. The effective use of technology reduces and/or eliminates many of the obstacles that hinder instruction and improves the teacher's ability to address the needs of all students.

Technology increases the frequency of assignment completion and contributes to improved motivation (Bahr, Nelson, and Van Meter, 1996). A key factor in technology implementation is collaboration between teachers, school staff, parents and students. This team can determine the devices best suited to assist each student's specific needs.

COMPETENCY 3   **KNOWLEDGE OF ASSESSMENT IN MATHEMATICS**

Skill 3.1   Assess student learning through various methods (e.g., informal, formative, summative)

Assessments in the classroom serve many purposes. They give students and teachers feedback, allowing both to make adjustments in order to enhance student learning. There are three types of assessments: diagnostic (such as pre-tests), formative, and summative. Diagnostic and formative assessments may be formal or informal, and are useful in planning instruction. Summative assessments are generally formal, and measure how well students have mastered what was taught.

Pre-assessments or pre-tests measure existing skills, can be used to gauge how ready students are to proceed to a particular topic or unit, and can be compared to post-unit tests to help measure students' progress. Formative assessments are used to tell how well students are learning material as a unit is being taught. Teachers can use formative assessments not only to adjust instruction to the class as a whole, but also to identify struggling students who may need individual intervention. Summative assessments measure what a student has learned at the end of an instructional unit, against a standard or benchmark.

Informal assessment: Informal assessment allows teachers to evaluate student progress on a regular basis. With informal assessment techniques, teachers can adjust instruction on the move to target specific areas where a student is having problems.

There are a multitude of informal assessment techniques available. A few examples:

Request an application example: After teaching a math topic, ask the students to write down a real-life application of what they learned. Students will establish a connection not only with real life applications but also with other content areas.

Brainstorming: Brainstorming is a spontaneous, informal group discussion. Encourage students to throw out ideas instead of concentrating on finding the "right" answer. It often gives teachers insight into what students know, or how they perceive a topic. It can be a useful tool to gauge what students know prior to more formal problem solving.

Checklists: Behavioral or content area objective oriented, checklists are a very effective tool to measure daily progress of students. Over time, it is a great tool to rate the progress of the student within the math curriculum.

Other informal methods include hand signals (thumbs up/down), journal entries, index card prompts (exit cards with summary of what you learned today), index card with listing things you don't quite understand from today, etc...

Some websites with informal assessment ideas:

http://www.theowlteacher.com/informal-assessments-list-ideas/

http://wvde.state.wv.us/schoolimprovement/documents/Informal_Assessment_Str
ategies.pdf

https://www.education.com/reference/article/informal-methods-assessment/

Formative assessment

Formative assessments include formal and informal methods. The purpose of formative assessment is to provide feedback on the effectiveness of instruction to both teacher and student, so that adjustments may be made. The defining characteristic of formative assessment is its interactive or cyclical nature (Sadler, 1988). Teachers adjust their instructions based on the information they collect from their classrooms. Formative assessment is only effective when the results of the assessment are used to analyze and respond to students' progress. The most common formative assessment procedures include Observation (teachers observe the student, comes up with a supporting plan and then determines its effectiveness), Self-assessment (students monitor their own progress), Feedback (teacher gives all kinds of feedback from responses to questions given in class to feedback on student work), and Curriculum-Based Measurement (CBM). Frequent and timely feedback to students is important so that they have opportunities to improve.

CBM is the most important group of standardized measures to determine student performance and to monitor their progress (Deno, 2001). The greatest benefit of using CBM is it creates a database not only for a student but also for a group. Math CBM focus is in developing estimation and fluency with facts. Estimation is used in daily life more than exact computation. Many results generated by estimation represent the outcome of numerous mathematic problems taught in middle school. Estimation is one of the most valuable skills in math. That is the reason that basic CBM tasks focus on estimation items that need to be done in a certain period of time. Multiple-choice items that include distracters are a good example of this. CBM also focuses in assessing fluency with facts because of the importance of gaining automaticity in basic skills as a foundation for gaining higher levels of math competence (Foegen and Deno, 2001).

Some examples of formative assessment techniques are found in these sites:

http://www.stma.k12.mn.us/documents/DW/Q_Comp/FormativeAssessStrategies
.pdf

http://www.levy.k12.fl.us/instruction/instructional_tools/60formativeassessment.p
df

http://cmrweb.gfps.k12.mt.us/uploads/2/7/3/6/27366965/formative_assessment_ppt.pdf

Summative assessment: Summative assessments are given at the end of a defined period, such as a unit, semester, or school year. The purpose of summative assessments are to determine how well a student has mastered what they were expected to learn. Student learning is measured against predefined targets or benchmarks.

Examples of this kind of assessment are:

- End of chapter, unit or semester project or test
- Standardized assessment to evaluate grade level expectations
- End of course grades
- Portfolios

Skill 3.2   Analyze student work samples to assess and diagnose student learning needs

Examining student work gives teachers   insight into students' understanding of concepts, aiding teachers in making decisions that improve student learning. Teachers design their instruction based on the curriculum, and then implement their plans. Frequent examination and analysis of student work is necessary to evaluate student learning, and adjust those instructional designs as needed.

Analysis of student work should be performed to both evaluate individual student learning and whole class learning. A common technique to assess whole class learning is to select work samples from three different students of varying abilities. Typically, a lower performing student, a medium performing student, and a higher performing student are chosen. If your class has English language learners, it is advisable to select an English language learner in addition.

In order for a meaningful analysis of student work to take place, learning objectives as well as assessment methods and performance criteria for these learning objectives must be established and communicated clearly to students. Teachers can then select and examine work samples. Analysis of selected work samples enables teachers to identify the next step in instruction by ascertaining how well students are meeting learning objectives.

As noted, this kind of analysis can be done for individual students and for the class as a whole. Individual student work analysis may help identify students who are struggling and need additional attention. For the class as a whole, look for trends or patterns in performance. For example, were there concepts or topics students understood well? Were there misconceptions, confusions, or a lack of complete understanding? Was the lesson too easy? Were there deficiencies in pre-requisite skills or knowledge? After reflection, use the analysis of this student work to make any adjustments in instruction needed to improve student learning.

Skill 3.3   Analyze student performance using technology (e.g., online resources, audience-response systems, instructor software)

Students' performance can be analyzed by traditional means and by using technology. There are multiple resources to make sense of performance data but technology is the faster and more secure way to organize, record and analyze scores from multiple student work samples.

In general, students who use computer-based instruction score better in tests compared to students without computers. Some students are more efficient, learning more in less time when they receive computer based instruction. Generally, students like their classes more when technology is used. This is not only limited to the learning process but also for assessments.

Instructor software: Teachers have a variety of software that allow them to store and analyze students' scores. Spreadsheet programs include Microsoft Excel © and OpenOffice Calc ©. Spreadsheets have a variety of mathematical functions that allow the user to perform data analysis, compare and contrast tasks and statistical measurements, which are the tools needed to make sense of multiple students' results. It also allows teachers to manage each student in a different way, to track their progress against their own customizable syllabus, to create tailored lesson diagrams and to make annotations to monitor the progress of each student. The most important part of integrating technology into the classroom is to develop essential 21st century skills for students and teachers.

Audience-response system (ARS): ARS's are hardware based, software based or, more commonly, a mix of both. In hardware based response systems, the teacher uses computers, video projectors and other hardware presentational tool to engage students in assessment activities. This system requires all students to have hardware (e.g. electronic pads) they will use to respond to multiple choice questions (e.g. pressing a button) presented by the teacher. Software based ARS develops questions and items presentation software that is later used in online tools and together with hardware in the classroom. The students can go to a computer station and access the questions in a variety of formats. Questions could be multiple choice, or open ended.

Online resources: One of the most important online resources to analyze student performance is the creation of Instructional Improvement Systems (IIS). IIS are tools that provide teachers with support for a cycle of instructional improvement that includes instructional planning, interim assessment and information analysis with the support of rapid-time reporting. IIS's provides online access to electronic curriculum, tools aligned with the standards, online formative assessment and data analysis capabilities, as well as early warning indicator for teachers, students and parents.

Other online resources include Parent portals in the school's website, where parents can monitor their children's progress.

Skill 3.4   Interpret student performance data to drive instruction

Student performance data plays a significant role in making good decisions about instruction. It is critical to know how to use that data. It is important to make that data part of the instructional improvement process.

Data use must have various sources and be part of a cyclic process that allows teachers to develop and implement strategies to improve students' performance. Teachers using data systems are able to share effective practices, adopt collective expectations for students' performance and have a better idea of the student's needs. The final goal is to design tailored strategies that optimally serve students.

Teachers must be able to explain to students clearly what their performance expectation will be, as well as assessment criteria. Provide feedback in a timely manner and appropriate format. Provide data analyzing tools to diagnose and handle feedback (e.g. reflective questions, teacher and students generated graphs). This will allow students to make correct data-driven decisions to improve their performance. Teachers will then be able to analyze student data to provide a more engaging and needs-driven instruction.

Skill 3.5   Recognize cognitive complexity in various questioning strategies

Students in Florida are assessed annually using the FSA (Florida Standards Assessments) and at the end of Algebra I, Geometry, and Algebra II with end of course (EOC) assessments. These assessments employ a depth of knowledge system developed by Dr. Norman L. Webb.

Dr. Webb's system can be used to judge the cognitive complexity (cognitive demand) of various assessment tasks, and can be applied as well to learning activities in the classroom. His method categorizes tasks into four levels of cognitive expectation needed to complete the task effectively. These levels are termed "depth of knowledge", or DOK. The higher the number of the DOK, the greater the cognitive demand. DOK levels are described as follows:

DOK 1   Recall & Reproduction
DOK 2   Skills & Concepts
DOK 3   Strategic Thinking & Reasoning
DOK 4   Extended Thinking

DOK 1: Recall and Reproduction

Tasks or questions in this level require the student only to recall or reproduce something, such as facts or simple formulas, or to complete a simple task. Examples include finding the area of a triangle or rectangle given a figure with the necessary dimensions labeled, solving a one-step word problem, remembering multiplication facts, using a ruler to measure an object, or solving a simple algebraic equation.

DOK 2: Skills and Concepts

Tasks or questions in this level require students to process information or knowledge before responding or proceeding. Students may be asked to describe cause and effect, make predictions, explain why. Examples include solving multi-step problems or equations, comparing and contrasting situations or problems, interpreting information from simple graphs, organizing data in a graph, making estimates, or recognizing a pattern in a group of numbers and adding new numbers that follow the pattern.

DOK 3: Strategic Thinking and Reasoning

Tasks or questions in this level require higher order thinking. They bring to mind words such as evaluation, analysis, planning, and synthesis. There may be more than one answer possible. Multiple skills may be required to solve a problem. Students may be asked to explain reasoning and support for their answers, or compare and contrast solution methods. Examples include interpreting information from complex graphs, solving multi-step problems or equation which have more than one decision point, constructing logical arguments (such as proofs), generating a mathematical model, making conjectures, or coming up with a descriptive rule for a pattern in a group of numbers.

DOK 4: Extended Thinking

Tasks or questions in this level require higher-level thinking and reasoning. Students may need to use skills from several curricular areas, solve problems over an extended period of time, solve open-ended problems, or adjust their approaches. Tasks may be project based, with a great deal of flexibility for methods and solutions. Examples include a project that requires identifying, analyzing, and solving a problem, designing and conducting experiments, or collecting data with multiple variables over an extended time, analyzing it, drawing conclusions, and presenting the results.

A few websites on cognitive complexity:

Depth of Knowledge
http://robertkaplinsky.com/tag/depth-of-knowledge-dok/

DOK for Cognitive Coding in 6-12 Mathematics
http://robertkaplinsky.com/depth-of-knowledge-examples-for-secondary-mathematics/

A Guide for Using Webb's Depth of Knowledge with Common Core State Standards
https://education.ohio.gov/getattachment/Topics/Teaching/Educator-Evaluation-System/How-to-Design-and-Select-Quality-Assessments/Webbs-DOK-Flip-Chart.pdf.aspx

Depth of Knowledge Levels for Mathematics
https://www.mais-web.org/uploaded/MSIS_Math_Institute/Math_V/Handouts_(Erma)/DOK_Math_rubric.pdf

Example:
One of Robert Kaplinsky's articles (first website listed above) illustrates how a problem might look at different DOK levels.

DOK 1: What is the perimeter of a rectangle that measures 8 units by 4 units?
DOK 2: List the dimensions of a rectangle with a perimeter of 24 units.
DOK 3: Of all the rectangles with a perimeter of 24 units, which one has the largest area?

Skill 3.6   Evaluate appropriate alternative assessments (e.g., projects, portfolios) that utilize various cognitive complexity levels

In addition to the traditional methods of performance assessment like multiple choice, true/false, and matching tests, there are many other assessment methods available to teachers. Alternative assessment is any type of assessment in which students create a response rather than choose an answer.

Short-response and essay questions are alternative methods of performance assessment. In responding to such questions, students must utilize verbal, graphical, and mathematical skills to construct answers to problems. These multifaceted responses allow the teacher to examine more closely a student's problem-solving and reasoning skills.

Student portfolios are another method of alternative assessment. In creating a portfolio, students collect samples of their work, self-assessments, and teacher evaluations over a period of time. Such a collection allows students, parents, and teachers to evaluate student progress and achievements. In addition, portfolios provide insight into a student's thought process and learning style.

Additionally, projects, demonstrations, and oral presentations are means of alternative assessment that require students to use different skills than those used on traditional tests. Such assessments require higher-order thinking, creativity, and the integration of reasoning and communication skills. The use of predetermined rubrics, with specific criteria for performance assessment, is the accepted method of evaluation for projects, demonstrations, and presentations.

COMPETENCY 4   **KNOWLEDGE OF CONNECTIONS AMONG MATHEMATICAL CONCEPTS**

Skill 4.1   Identify prerequisite skills for a given topic

A popular theory of math learning is constructivism. Constructivists argue that prior knowledge greatly influences the learning of math, and learning is cumulative and vertically structured. Instruction must build on the innate knowledge of students and address any common misconceptions. Thus, it is important for teachers to ensure that students possess the prerequisite knowledge and ideas required to learn a particular topic. Even without an appeal to constructivism, it is obvious that a student who does not understand the concept of percentage will not be able to do a problem involving interest rates.

In order to identify the prerequisite skills needed to solve a particular kind of problem, the broad concepts that underlie the problem must first be identified. For each concept, one can then list the specific skills needed to perform the related mathematical operations. This kind of hierarchical analysis may be summarized in a tree diagram as shown below.

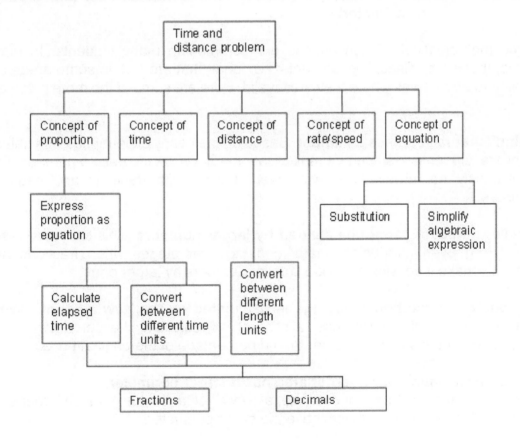

The above analysis can be done in different ways. The essential idea is to identify all the pieces that go into learning a topic.

Teachers can gain insight into the prior knowledge of students by beginning each lesson with open-ended questions that allow students to share their thoughts and ideas on the subject or topic.

A short pre-test covering the prerequisite topics can also be useful as an assessment tool.

Once gaps and weaknesses in students' prerequisite knowledge are identified, the teacher will need to review those topics before teaching new content. This can be accomplished through discussion or written exercises, as well as through hands-on activities.

Example: When teaching a unit on the geometry of three-dimensional solids, teachers can ask students to design a structure of his/her choice using solids. This exercise allows students to explore, discover and apply the properties, including surface area, vertices, edges and volume, of solids.

Skill 4.2   Identify common misconceptions in mathematics (e.g. area and perimeter)

Some mathematical misconceptions are common to many students. In many cases, these are misapplied concepts; i.e. ideas that are true in some areas are applied to other areas where they are invalid. Here are some of the more prevalent ones:

Multiplication increases a number. Based on their early experiences with natural numbers, students assume that multiplication will always increase a number. This is obviously not always the case when dealing with fractions and negative numbers.

Smaller numbers cannot be divided by larger numbers. This too is the result of carrying over introductory math ideas to later stages when fractions and decimals make it possible to divide smaller numbers by larger ones.

Percentage or fraction of change is calculated on the new amount. While figuring a discount, for instance, a student will calculate the percentage as a percentage of the sale price rather than a percentage of the original price.

A geometric figure with a larger area has a larger perimeter.
This is not generally true. For example, a 10"x4" rectangle has a much larger area than a 12"x2" rectangle but both have the same perimeter.

Square or cubic units have the same conversion factor as the single unit.
Some students assume that 1sq.m. = 100 sq.cm. just because 1 m = 100 cm.

A number raised to an exponent is the same as the number multiplied by the exponent. E.g. $x^3 = 3x$. This error is probably due to verbal descriptions of x^3 as 3 x's multiplied together.

Unclear meaning of a variable in algebra word problem. A word problem is set up, for instance, so that x stands for the number of pencils. At some point in the problem, the student switches to treating x as if it is the price of a pencil. This is due to an imprecise association of x with pencil without clearly defining which property of "pencil" x represents.

Skill 4.3   Connect interrelated mathematical concepts (e.g. scale factor and proportional reasoning)

Recognition and understanding of the relationships between concepts and topics is important to mathematical problem solving and the explanation of more complex processes. It becomes much easier for a student to retain information when it is presented from different viewpoints and linked to other familiar concepts. Ideally, a teacher will not present the information straight away but will let students think for themselves and discover the connections on their own with guidance from the teacher. Some examples of connections between familiar mathematical concepts are discussed below.

Multiplication is simply repeated addition. This relationship explains the concept of variable addition.

We can show that the expression $4x + 3x = 7x$ is true by rewriting 4 times x and 3 times x as repeated addition, yielding the expression $(x + x + x + x) + (x + x + x)$. Thus, because of the relationship between multiplication and addition, variable addition is accomplished by coefficient addition.

Addition and subtraction are really the same operation acting in opposite directions on the number line. Understanding this concept helps students in working with negative numbers, which are difficult for many middle-school children to grasp.

The concept of **rate appears in many different guises** in mathematics such as in the speed of a vehicle, interest rate or the price per unit of an item. The concept of rate is also directly connected to the concept of slope of a straight line.

Commonly used formulas such as $a^2 - b^2 = (a+b)(a-b)$ or $(a+b)^2 = a^2 + 2ab + b^2$ are not magical relationships that need to be memorized. They can simply be calculated by performing the familiar **FOIL** operation.

Example: $(a+b)(a-b) = a^2 - ab + ba - b^2 = a^2 - b^2$

In geometry, the perimeters, areas and volumes of different figures are usually presented as separate formulas. It is useful to point out that every **area contains the product of two lengths** (e.g., *lw* or πr^2) and every **volume contains the product of three lengths** (e.g., l^3 or $\pi r^2 h$). This helps students understand the meaning of square and cubic units.

The relationships between points, lines and planes become easier to visualize if one understands that **a point is to a line as a line is to a plane**. Just as two lines intersect in a point, two planes intersect in a line.

Application of a **scale factor** is related to **proportional reasoning**. A scale drawing, such as a map that is "drawn to scale," is a representation of an object or region that is proportionally identical to that which it represents. Thus, for instance, a scale drawing (map) of a city is like a picture that has been reduced in size; distances between points on the map are a specified fraction of the distances between the points in reality. (For instance, the distance between two parks may be 2,000 feet, but a map that uses a scale of 1:24,000 or, similarly, inch = 1,000 feet would show this distance as 1 inch.) By maintaining this proportion consistent for the distances between any two points on the map, the drawing is made to scale.

Example: The scale on a map is 1 inch = 6 miles. What is the actual distance between two cities if they are 3 inches apart on the map?

Write a proportion comparing the scale to the actual distance.

$$\text{scale / actual:} \quad 1/6 = 3/x$$
$$\text{cross multiply:} \quad 1x = 3 \cdot 6$$
$$x = 18$$

Thus, the actual distance between the cities is 18 miles. The answer can also be found by applying the scale *factor* of 6: $3 \cdot 6 = 18$.

Students can discover many more connections in the classroom with the teacher's help. This will not only enhance the quality of their learning but will also make them better and more eager learners.

Skill 4.4   Analyze mathematical errors, including computation, algebraic, data analysis, and geometric errors

Successful teachers need to be able to identify multiple types of student errors. A simple method for analyzing student errors is to ask how the answer was obtained. The teacher can then determine which step or misinterpretation has resulted in the wrong answer. There is value to having the students explain how they arrived at the correct, as well as incorrect, answers.

A teacher should be aware that many students' computational skills exceed their reading level and they stumble on interpreting the **language** in word problems and in directions. Although they understand basic operations, they fail to grasp the concept or to understand the question completely.

If a teacher is familiar with some common student errors, mistakes can be more easily identified. Additionally, the curriculum can be tailored to help students recognize and reduce the frequency of these errors. The following are some of the common errors committed by students.

<u>Common computation errors:</u>

1. Failing to line up place values and decimal points correctly.

$$\text{Example: } \begin{array}{r} 125 \\ +50 \\ \hline 175 \end{array} \text{ (not } \begin{array}{r} 125 \\ +50 \\ \hline 625 \end{array} \text{)}$$

2. Moving decimal points in the wrong direction when multiplying or dividing.

<u>Example:</u>
$0.125 \div 1000 = 0.000125$ (**not** $0.125 \div 1000 = 125$)

3. Not expressing fractions with common denominators when adding or subtracting.

<u>Example:</u> $\dfrac{1}{5} + \dfrac{4}{15} = \dfrac{3}{15} + \dfrac{4}{15} = \dfrac{7}{15}$ (**not** $\dfrac{1}{5} + \dfrac{4}{15} = \dfrac{5}{15}$)

4. Not using parentheses correctly, particularly with negative numbers.

<u>Example:</u>
$(-3) \times (-3) = (-3)^2 = 9$ **not** $(-3) \times (-3) = -3^2 = -9$

5. Canceling mistakes such as canceling only one of the terms in the numerator of a fraction.

<u>Example:</u> $\dfrac{12 \times 4 + 6}{4} = 12 + \dfrac{6}{4}$ **not** $\dfrac{12 \times 4 + 6}{4} = 12 + 6$

Common algebra errors:

1. Failing to distribute:

   Example: $4x - (2x - 3) = 4x - 2x + 3$ **not** $4x - 2x - 3$
   Example: $3(2x + 5) = 6x + 15$ **not** $6x + 5$

2. Distributing exponents:

   Example: $(x + y)^2 = x^2 + 2xy + y^2$ **not** $x^2 + y^2$

3. Canceling terms instead of factors:
   Example: $\dfrac{x^3 + 5}{x} = x^2 + \dfrac{5}{x}$ **not** $x^2 + 5$

4. Misunderstanding negative and fractional exponents:

   Example: $x^{\frac{1}{2}} = \sqrt{x}$ **not** $\dfrac{1}{x^2}$

   Example: $x^{-2} = \dfrac{1}{x^2}$ **not** $\sqrt{x}$

5. Neglecting to follow the order of operations:

   Example: $2 + 6 - 9 \times 2 = -10$ **not** -2

Teachers also must not neglect multiple errors in the work of a student that may be disguised by a correct answer. For example, failing twice to properly distribute negative one in the following arithmetic operation produces a deceptively correct answer.

(Remind students that it helps to place parentheses around multiplication and division operations.)

Example:

$4x-(2x+3)-(2x-3) = 4x-2x+3-2x-3 = 0$ (incorrect distribution)

$4x-(2x+3)-(2x-3) = 4x-2x-3-2x+3 = 0$ (correct distribution)

Common data analysis errors:

1. Not ordering a set of numbers accurately.

   Example: For data set 1,6,8,2,9,5,4,7,6, the median is 6 (**not** 9).

2. Counting data points more than once.

   Example: In creating a frequency distribution of a data set, putting boundary values in both adjoining bins.

   Data set: 2,3,3,5,6,7,9,10,12,12,16.

Range	No. of points
0-5	3
5-10	4
10-15	3
15-20	1

   (counting points less than the upper bound of range) or

Range	No. of points
0-5	4
5-10	4
10-15	2
15-20	1

   (including upper bound of range) but **not** the following

Range	No. of points
0-5	4
5-10	5
10-15	3
15-20	1

   (The data set appears to have 13 data points instead of 11)

3. Confusing the meanings of commonly used terms such as percentile and percentage.

   Example: A group of students scored the following points on a test out of a possible total of 100: 30, 53, 65, 72, 80, 75.

   How many students scored above the 50th percentile?
   Answer: 3 (**not** 5)

Common geometry errors:

1. Using perception instead of reasoning.

    Example: Find the area of the shaded region in the figure below.

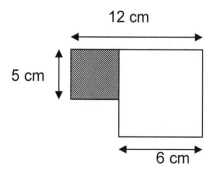

    Area = 5 x 6 = 30 sq. cm. (**not** 25 sq. cm. because the area appears to be square)

2. Inability to visualize different parts of plane or three-dimensional figures. Some students will be unable to solve the following problem without a formula.

    Example: What is the area of the paper that will be needed to completely cover all surfaces of a box with length 10 in, width 5 inches and height 3 inches.

    A box has 6 surfaces.

    Two rectangular surfaces will have area 10 in. x 5 in.
    Two rectangular surfaces will have area 5 in. x 3 in.
    Two rectangular surfaces will have area 3 in. x 10 in.
    Total area = 100 + 30 + 60 = 190 sq. in.

Students need to be taught that making mistakes is a part of the learning process. Teachers should encourage students to keep positive attitude so the students do not feel defeated or frustrated.

Skill 4.5   Identify fundamental ideas that connect middle grades mathematics to advanced mathematics (e.g., trigonometry, number theory, pre-calculus, calculus)

Middle school mathematics lays the groundwork for the progression of concrete ideas mastered in the elementary years to less concrete, more algebraic understandings of mathematical ideas. As students progress to later grades, the concepts are more deeply developed and connections between the various skills become more apparent. Skills developed in middle school are part of the progression of skills that begins formally in the primary grades and continues afterwards into high school and beyond.

In middle school, students are developing their **number sense**, focusing mainly on decimals, fractions, proportion, roots and negative numbers. A clear understanding of these ideas is essential, as their task in high school years is to understand how numeration concepts relate to each other. **Estimation** is largely a rote pen and paper skill in middle school years, but in high school and beyond, estimation is strongly geared around evaluating the reasonableness of answers using the understanding developed in middle school. Sophisticated calculators are utilized in high school in ways involving calculated rounding, either user-defined or part of the calculator's programming. For this reason, the high school student needs to be able to recognize the reasonableness of the outcomes of functions when calculated on a calculator.

The analysis **of relationships or functions** progresses to more algebraic forms in middle school, but the skill of developing models to demonstrate patterns and functions must also be maintained. In high school and beyond, students extend their understanding of functions to include the symbolic ideas of domain, range, and *f(x)* notation. Both the concrete and symbolic understandings of functions are used in advanced mathematics. Many careers including engineering and architecture rely on the use and analysis of concrete working models.

Calculus mainly involves the study of limit, rate of change, area under a curve, and slope of a tangent line. In middle school, the base work for these concepts is developed. Students develop an understanding for infinity, linear growth, exponential growth, slope, and change over time. High school level pre-calculus is generally aimed at developing understanding of main calculus concepts. More specific calculus techniques such as differentiation and convergence testing are generally reserved for college-level mathematics.

Trigonometry is a branch of mathematics dealing with angles, triangles, and the functions sine, cosine and tangent. Two aspects of trigonometry developed in middle school are geometrical knowledge (e.g. similar triangles, the Pythagorean Theorem) and algebraic skills (e.g. solving equations and using algebraic expressions). Trigonometry is adapted into careers involving astronomy, land surveying, and acoustics, among a wide array of others.

COMPETENCY 5   **KNOWLEDGE OF NUMBER SENSE, OPERATIONS, AND PROPORTIONALITY**

Skill 5.1   **Compare the relative size of real numbers expressed in a variety of forms, including fractions, decimals, percents, and scientific notation**

Mathematical manipulation often involves converting real numbers from one form to another for convenience of calculation or ease of interpretation. For instance, test scores may be easier to compute using decimals but easier to understand when represented as percentages. The representation may also be dictated by the size of the number. Scientific notation is used to represent very large or very small numbers. In some instances, one may need to compare two numbers expressed in different forms. In this case, one of the numbers must be converted to the other form.

To convert a **fraction to a decimal**, simply divide the numerator (top) by the denominator (bottom). Use long division if necessary.

Example: Find the decimal equivalent of $\frac{7}{10}$.

$$
\begin{array}{r}
0.7 \\
10\overline{)7.0} \\
\underline{70} \\
00
\end{array}
$$

Since 10 cannot divide into 7 evenly, put a decimal point in the answer row on top; put a zero behind 7 to make it 70. Continue the division process. If a remainder occurs, put a zero by the last digit of the remainder and continue the division. Thus $\frac{7}{10} = 0.7$

It is a good idea to write a zero before the decimal point so that the decimal point is emphasized.

Example: Find the decimal equivalent of $\frac{7}{125}$.

$$
\begin{array}{r}
0.056 \\
125\overline{)7.000} \\
\underline{625} \\
750 \\
\underline{750} \\
0
\end{array}
$$

If a decimal has a fixed number of digits, the decimal is said to be terminating. To write such a **decimal as a fraction**, first determine what place value the farthest right digit is in, for example: tenths, hundredths, thousandths, ten thousandths, hundred thousands, etc. Then drop the decimal and place the string of digits over the number given by the place value. One can also think of this operation as multiplying by 1 in the form of a fraction (e.g., $\frac{10}{10}, \frac{100}{100}, \frac{1000}{1000}$) to get rid of the decimal point.

Example: Convert 0.056 to a fraction.

Multiplying 0.056 by $\frac{1000}{1000}$ to get rid of the decimal point

$$0.056 \times \frac{1000}{1000} = \frac{56}{1000} = \frac{7}{125}$$

If a decimal continues forever by repeating a string of digits, the decimal is said to be repeating. To write a **repeating decimal as a fraction**, follow these steps.

1. Let x = the repeating decimal
    (e.g. x=0.716716716...)

2. Multiply x by the multiple of ten that will move the decimal just to the right of the repeating block of digits.
    (e.g. 1000x=716.716716...)

3. Subtract the first equation from the second.
    $(e.g.\ 1000x - x = 716.716716\ldots. -0.716716)$

4. Simplify and solve this equation. The repeating block of digits will subtract out.
    (e.g., $999x = 716$ so $x = \frac{716}{999}$)
    The solution will be the fraction for the repeating decimal.

A **decimal can be converted to a percent** by multiplying by 100%, or merely moving the decimal point two places to the right. A **percent can be converted to a decimal** by dividing by 100%, or moving the decimal point two places to the left.

Examples: Convert the following decimals into percents.

> 0.375 = 37.5%
> 0.7 = 70%
> 0.04 = 4 %
> 3.15 = 315 %

Examples: Convert the following percents into decimals.

$$84\% = 0.84$$
$$3\% = 0.03$$
$$60\% = 0.6$$
$$110\% = 1.1$$
$$0.5\% = 0.005$$

A **percent can be converted to a fraction** by placing it over 100 and reducing to simplest terms.

Examples: Convert the following percents into fractions.

$$32\% = \frac{32}{100} = \frac{8}{25}$$
$$6\% = \frac{6}{100} = \frac{3}{50}$$
$$111\% = \frac{111}{100} = 1\frac{11}{100}$$
$$10\% = \frac{10}{100} = \frac{1}{10}$$

The **percentage** of a number can be found by converting the percentage into decimal form and then multiplying the decimal by the number.

Example: Find 23% of 1000.
$$23\% = 0.23$$
$$0.23 \times 1000 = 230$$

Scientific notation is a more convenient method for writing very large and very small numbers. It employs two factors. The first factor is a number between -10 and 10. The second factor is a power of 10. This notation is a shorthand way to express large numbers (like the weight of 100 freight cars in kilograms) or small numbers (like the weight of an atom in grams).

Recall:

$10^n = (10)^n$	Ten multiplied by itself n times.
$10^6 = 1,000,000$	(mega)
$10^3 = 10 \times 10 \times 10 = 1000$	(kilo)
$10^2 = 10 \times 10 = 100$	(hecto)
$10^1 = 10$	(deca)
$10^0 = 1$	Any nonzero number raised to power of zero is 1.
$10^{-1} = 1/10$	(deci)
$10^{-2} = 1/100$	(centi)
$10^{-3} = 1/1000$	(milli)

$10^{-6} = 1/1,000,000$ (micro)

Scientific notation format

Convert a number to a form of $b \times 10^n$ where -10 < b < 10 and n is an integer.

Example: 356.73 can be written in various forms.

$$356.73 = 3567.3 \times 10^{-1} \quad (1)$$
$$= 35673 \times 10^{-2} \quad (2)$$
$$= 35.673 \times 10^{1} \quad (3)$$
$$= 3.5673 \times 10^{2} \quad (4)$$
$$= 0.35673 \times 10^{3} \quad (5)$$

Only (4) is written in proper scientific notation format.

Example: Write 46,368,000 in scientific notation.

1) Introduce a decimal point. 46,368,000 = 46,368,000.0
2) Move the decimal place to the **left** until only one nonzero digit is in front of it, in this case between the 4 and 6.
3) Count the number of digits the decimal point moved, in this case 7. This is the nth the power of ten and is **positive** because the decimal point moved **left**.

Therefore, $46,368,000 = 4.6368 \times 10^{7}$

Example: Write 0.00397 in scientific notation.

1) Decimal point is already in place.
2) Move the decimal point to the **right** until there is only one nonzero digit in front of it, in this case between the 3 and 9.
3) Count the number of digits the decimal point moved, in this case 3. This is the nth the power of ten and is **negative** because the decimal point moved **right**.

Therefore, $0.00397 = 3.97 \times 10^{-3}$.

Example: Evaluate $\dfrac{3.22\times10^{-3}\times736}{0.00736\times32.2\times10^{-6}}$

Since we have a mixture of large and small numbers, convert each number to scientific notation:

$$736 = 7.36\times10^2$$

$$0.00736 = 7.36\times10^{-3}$$

$32.2\times10^{-6} = 3.22\times10^{-5}$ thus we have, $\dfrac{3.22\times10^{-3}\times7.36\times10^2}{7.36\times10^{-3}\times3.22\times10^{-5}}$

$$= \dfrac{3.22\times7.36\times10^{-3}\times10^{2}}{7.36\times3.22\times10^{-3}\times10^{-5}}$$

$$= \dfrac{3.22\times7.36}{7.36\times3.22}\times\dfrac{10^{-1}}{10^{-8}}$$

$$= \dfrac{3.22\times7.36}{3.22\times7.36}\times10^{-1}\times10^8$$

$$= \dfrac{23.6992}{23.6992}\times10^7$$

$$= 1\times10^7 = 10,000,000$$

Skill 5.2 Apply mental computation and identify estimation strategies

Estimation and approximation may be used to check the reasonableness of answers. This is particularly important when calculators are used. Students need to be able to verify that the answer they are getting by punching in numbers is in the correct range and makes sense in the given context. Estimation requires good mental math skills. There are several different ways of estimating.

A simple check for reasonableness is to ask whether the answer expected is **more or less** than a given number. It is astonishing how many errors of computation can be avoided using this method. For instance, when converting 20 Km to meters, ask whether you are expecting a number greater or less than 20. That will tell you whether to multiply or divide by 1000 (a common point of confusion in conversion problems).

The most common estimation strategies taught in schools involve replacing numbers with ones that are simpler to compute. These methods include **rounding off**, **front-end digit estimation** and **compensation**. While rounding off is done to a specific place value (e.g. nearest ten or hundred), front-end estimation involves rounding off or truncating to whatever place value the first digit in a number represents. The following example uses front-end estimation.

Example: Estimate the answer.

$$\frac{58 \times 810}{1989}$$

58 becomes 60, 810 becomes 800 and 1989 becomes 2000.

$$\frac{60 \times 800}{2000} = 24$$

Compensation involves replacing different numbers in different ways so that one change can more or less compensate for the other.

Example: 32+ 53=30+55=85

Here, both numbers are replaced in a way that minimizes the change; one number is increased and the other is decreased.

Another estimation strategy is to **estimate a range** for the correct answer.

Example: 458+873 > 400 + 800 and 458+873 < 500 + 900.

One can estimate that the sum of 458 and 873 lies in the range 1200 to 1400.

Converting to an **equivalent fraction, decimal or percentage** can often be helpful.

Example: To calculate 25% of 520, realize that 25%=1/4 and simply divide 520 by 4 to get 130.

Clustering is a useful strategy when dealing with a set of numbers. Similar numbers can be clubbed together to simplify computation.

Example: 1210 + 655 + 1178 + 683 + 628 + 1223 + 599 = 600 + 600 + 600 + 600 + 1200 + 1200 + 1200 = 2400 + 3600 = 6000.

Clubbing together **compatible numbers** is a variant of clustering. Here, instead of similar numbers, numbers that together produce easy to compute numbers are clubbed together.

Example: 5 + 17 + 25 + 23 + 40 = (5+25) + (17+23) + 40 = 30 + 40 + 40 = 110

Often a problem does not require exact computation. An estimate may sometimes be all that is needed to solve a word problem as in the example below. Therefore, **assessing what level of precision is needed** in a particular situation is an important skill that must be taught to all students.

Example: Janet goes into a store to purchase a CD on sale for $13.95. While shopping, she sees two pairs of shoes, prices $19.95 and $14.50. She only has $50. Can she purchase everything? (Assume there is no sales tax.)

Solve by rounding up to the nearest dollar:

$19.95 → $20.00
$14.50 → $15.00
$13.95 → $14.00
$49.00 Yes, she can purchase the CD and both pairs of shoes.

Skill 5.3   Apply prime factorization of composite numbers to other operations (e.g. cube roots, polynomials)

Prime numbers are numbers whose only factors are 1 and the number itself. When factoring into prime factors, all the factors must be numbers that cannot be factored again (without using 1).

Composite numbers are whole numbers that have more than 2 different factors. For example, 9 is composite because besides factors of 1 and 9, 3 is also a factor. 70 is also composite because besides the factors of 1 and 70, the numbers 2,5,7,10,14, and 35 are also all factors.

Through **prime factorization,** composite numbers are factored repeatedly until only prime numbers remain. First factor the composite number into any 2 factors. Check each resulting factor to see if it can be factored again. Continue factoring until all remaining factors are prime. This is the list of prime factors. Regardless of initial 2 factors, the final list of prime factors will always be the same.

Example: Factor 30 into prime factors.
Factor 30 into any 2 factors.

$5 \cdot 6$ Now factor the 6
$5 \cdot 2 \cdot 3$ These are all prime factors

Factor 30 into another 2 factors.

$3 \cdot 10$ Now factor the 10
$3 \cdot 2 \cdot 5$ These are the same prime factors

Note: Even though the initial 2 factors were different, the prime factors were the same.

Example: Factor 240 into prime factors.
Factor 240 into any 2 factors.

$24 \cdot 10$ Now factor both 24 and 10.
$4 \cdot 6 \cdot 2 \cdot 5$ Now factor both 4 and 6.
$2 \cdot 2 \cdot 2 \cdot 3 \cdot 2 \cdot 5$ These are prime factors.

This can also be written as $2^4 \cdot 3 \cdot 5$.

Using a number's prime factorization is an essential concept used within many simplification procedures in mathematics. For instance, finding two identical factors in a square root, three in a cube root, and so on, is a necessary step in the process of simplifying roots of numbers. To illustrate:

$$\sqrt{50} = \sqrt{2*5*5} = 5\sqrt{2} \text{ and } \sqrt[3]{54} = \sqrt[3]{2*3*3*3} = 3\sqrt[3]{2}$$

Additional examples concerning the simplification of radical expressions can be found in Skill 6.3

An understanding of prime factorization of numbers is also required when factoring the greatest common factor out of a polynomial.

$12x + 6y + 30z + 66 =$ $2 \bullet 2 \bullet 3x + 2 \bullet 3y + 2 \bullet 3 \bullet 5z + 2 \bullet 3 \bullet 11$
$2 \bullet 3(2x + y + 5z + 11)$
$6(2x + y + 5z + 11)$

Furthermore, prime factorization is used in computations and simplifications of rational numbers. (See Skill 5.4) Looking at a composite number's prime factorization allows for a sound basis of comparison or combination with other numbers and operations.

Skill 5.4 **Compute fluently with rational numbers using the greatest common factor (GCF) and least common multiple (LCM)**

The **greatest common factor (GCF)** is the largest number that is a factor of all the numbers given in a problem. The GCF can be no larger than the smallest number given in the problem. If no other number is a common factor, then the GCF will be the number 1. To find the GCF, list all possible factors of the smallest number given (include the number itself). Starting with the largest factor (which is the number itself), determine if it is also a factor of all the other given numbers. If so, that is the GCF. If that factor does not work, try the same method on the next smaller factor. Continue until a common factor is found. That is the GCF. Note: There can be other common factors besides the GCF.

Example: Find the GCF of 12, 20, and 36.

The smallest number in the problem is 12. The factors of 12 are 1, 2, 3, 4, 6, and 12. The largest factor is 12, but it does not divide evenly into 20. Neither does 6, but 4 will divide into both 20 and 36 evenly. Therefore, 4 is the GCF.

Example: Find the GCF of 14 and 15.

Factors of 14 are 1, 2, 7, and 14. The largest factor is 14, but it does not divide evenly into 15. Neither does 7 or 2. Therefore, the only factor common to both 14 and 15 is 1, the GCF.

The **least common multiple (LCM)** of a group of numbers is the smallest number into which all of the given numbers will divide. The least common multiple will always be the largest of the given numbers or a multiple of the largest number.

Example: Find the LCM of 20, 30, and 40.

The largest number given is 40, but 30 will not divide evenly into 40. The next multiple of 40 is 80 (2 x 40), but 30 will not divide evenly into 80 either. The next multiple of 40 is 120. 120 is divisible by both 20 and 30, so 120 is the LCM (least common multiple).

Example: Find the LCM of 96, 16, and 24.

The largest number is 96. The number 96 is divisible by both 16 and 24, so 96 is the LCM.

A strong grasp of GCFs and LCMs helps students work more successfully with rational numbers. For instance, when reducing a fraction, the GCF is the number to divide out, or the amount by which to reduce the fraction.

Example: Reduce 12/42. The GCF of 12 and 42 is 6. (6•2)/(6•7) means the fraction reduces to 2/7.

If the numerator and the denominator have no GCF other than 1, the fraction is already simplified, or in lowest terms.

Example: 8/15 is a fraction that is already reduced since 8 and 15 share no common factors other than 1.

Rational number addition relies on the distributive property of multiplication over addition and the understanding that multiplication of any number by one yields the same number. Consider the addition of 1/4 to 1/3 by means of common denominator. The best common denominator to create is the LCM. In the case of denominators 3 and 4, the LCM is 12.

Example:

$$\frac{1}{4}+\frac{1}{3}=\frac{3}{3}(\frac{1}{4})+\frac{4}{4}(\frac{1}{3})=(\frac{3}{12})+(\frac{4}{12})=\frac{7}{12} \quad \longrightarrow \quad \text{Recognize that } \frac{3}{3} \text{ and } \frac{4}{4} \text{ both equal 1.}$$

A common error in rational number addition is the failure to find a common denominator and adding both numerators and denominators.

Example:

$$\frac{1}{4}+\frac{1}{3}\neq\frac{2}{7}$$

The main algorithm of rational number division is multiplication by the reciprocal. Thus,

$$\frac{\frac{1}{3}}{\frac{1}{4}}=(\frac{1}{3})(\frac{4}{1})=\frac{4}{3}.$$

The definition of multiplication and division as inverse operations justifies the use of reciprocal multiplication.

Skill 5.5 Apply ratios and proportions to similar figures and to solve realistic problems

Proportions can be used to solve word problems whenever relationships are compared. Some situations which use proportions are scale drawings and maps, similar polygons, speed, time and distance, cost, and comparison shopping.

Example: Which is the better buy, 6 items for $1.29 or 8 items for $1.69?

Set up a proportion.

$$\frac{\$1.29}{6}=\frac{x}{1} \qquad\qquad \frac{\$1.69}{8}=\frac{x}{1}$$

Cross multiply.

$6x = \$1.29 \qquad\qquad 8x = \$1.69$

Isolate x.

$x = \$0.215/\text{item} \qquad\qquad x = \$0.21125/\text{item}$

Thus, 8 items for $1.69 is the better buy.

Example: A car travels 125 miles in 2.5 hours. How far will it go in 6 hours?

Write a proportion comparing the distance and time. $\dfrac{125 \text{ miles}}{2.5 \text{ hours}} = \dfrac{x}{6 \text{ hours}}$

Cross multiply.
(2.5 hours) x = 750 miles x hours

Divide both sides by 2.5 hours (the hours cancel out).
x = 300 miles

Thus, the car can travel 300 miles in 6 hours.

Example: The scale on a map is $\frac{3}{4}$ inch=6miles. What is the actual distance between two cities if they are $1\frac{1}{2}$ inches apart on the map?

Write a proportion comparing the scale distance to the actual distance.

scale actual
$\dfrac{\frac{3}{4}\text{in.}}{1\frac{1}{2}\text{in.}} = \dfrac{6 \text{ miles}}{x}$

Cross multiply.
$(\frac{3}{4}\text{in.})x=(1\frac{1}{2}\text{in.})(6 \text{ miles})$

Divide both sides by $\frac{3}{4}$ in. and multiply x = 12 miles

Thus, the actual distance between the cities is 12 miles.

Proportions may be used to perform indirect measurements. If it is known that two triangles are similar, the fact that their sides are related by the same proportion may be used to derive the measurements of one triangle from the other.

Example: In the diagram below, X represents the distance between two points with an unknown length. If the two triangles shown are similar, find X.

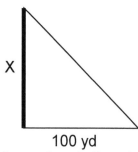

100 yd

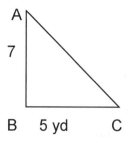

If the dimensions of a similar triangle are known, the problem can be solved by setting up the proportion below and solving for X.

$$\frac{X}{100 \text{ yd}} = \frac{7 \text{ yd}}{5 \text{ yd}}$$

After cross-multiplying, the equation can be written as 5X = 700; X equals 140 yards. Without actually measuring the distance with a measuring tape or other tool, the distance is determined.

Example: An architect is creating a scale drawing of a quadrilateral lot. The lot and the drawing are similar. Find the missing lengths of sides *x, y,* and *z.*

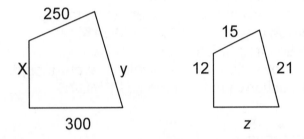

Since corresponding sides are proportional, find the scale used by the architect.

$^{250}/_{15} = {}^X/_{12}$	$^{250}/_{15} = {}^y/_{21}$	$^{250}/_{15} = {}^{300}/_z$
$15X = 3000$	$15y = 5250$	$250z = 4500$
$X = 200$	$y = 350$	$z = 18$

Skill 5.6   Select the appropriate operation(s) to solve realistic problems that involve real numbers

When selecting appropriate operations, students need to consider how the vocabulary and circumstances influence a problem as well as to consider how subsequent steps reflect appropriate operations. For instance, if a student encounters a problem where the mean or average is needed for a set of data, he or she uses the operations of addition and division. However, within those steps, the proper order needs to be preserved. Note the following two paths to an answer:

Find the average of: 42, 48, 59, 65

Technique 1) 42 + 48 + 59 + 65 = 214, 214 ÷ 4 = 53.5
Technique 2) 42 + 48 + 59 + 65 ÷ 4 = 165.25 (incorrect)

The answer for Technique 2 is incorrect because the answer is too large: the average should be within the range of the data. Further investigation into the second answer reveals that division was only performed on the 65, rather than the total of the 4 numbers. This student most likely failed to follow order of operations, a key element to proper problem solving.

The Order of Operations is used to evaluate algebraic expressions. Remember the mnemonic PEMDAS (Please Excuse My Dear Aunt Sally) to follow these steps in order:

1. Simplify inside grouping characters such as **p**arentheses, brackets, radicals, fraction bars, etc.
2. Multiply out expressions with **e**xponents.
3. Do **m**ultiplication or **d**ivision from left to right.
    Note: Multiplication and division are equivalent even though multiplication is mentioned before division in the mnemonic PEMDAS.
4. Do **a**ddition or **s**ubtraction from left to right.
    Note: Addition and subtraction are equivalent even though addition is mentioned before subtraction in the mnemonic PEMDAS.

Example: Evaluate $\dfrac{12(9-7)+4\cdot5}{3^4+2^3}$

$$\frac{12(9-7)+4\cdot5}{3^4+2^3}$$

$$=\frac{12(2)+4\cdot5}{3^4+2^3}\quad\text{Simplify within parenthesis}$$

$$=\frac{12(2)+4\cdot5}{81+8}\quad\text{Multiply out exponent expressions}$$

$$=\frac{24+20}{81+8}\quad\text{Do multiplication and division}$$

$$=\frac{44}{89}\quad\text{Do addition and subtraction}$$

Example: Evaluate $13(-10)^2+45\div(-5)$

$$13(-10)^2+45\div(-5)$$
$$=13(100)+45\div(-5)$$
$$=1300-9$$
$$=1291$$

Example: Evaluate $\dfrac{(-5)^2 - 4 \cdot 5}{3^2 + 4 \cdot 2(-1)^5}$

$$\dfrac{(-5)^2 - 4 \cdot 5}{3^2 + 4 \cdot 2(-1)^5}$$

$$= \dfrac{25 - 4 \cdot 5}{9 - 4 \cdot 2}$$

$$= \dfrac{25 - 20}{9 - 8}$$

$$= 5$$

Real world mathematical problems are solved in various sections throughout this guide (See **Skills 1.1, 5.5, 6.8, 7.6, and 9.7**. Following are several examples of realistic problems using percentages.)

Example: The Ski Club has 85 members. Eighty percent of the members are able to attend the meeting. How many members attended the meeting?

> Restate the problem: What is 80% of 85?
> Write an equation: $n = 0.8 \times 85$
> Solve: $n = 68$

Sixty-eight members attended the meeting.

Example: There are 64 dogs in the kennel. Forty-eight are collies. What percent are collies?

> Restate the problem: 48 is what percent of 64?
> Write an equation: $48 = n \times 64$
> Solve: $\frac{48}{64} = n$
>
> $n = \frac{3}{4} \times 100 = 75\%$

75% of the dogs are collies.

Example: The auditorium was filled to 90% capacity. There were 558 seats occupied. What is the capacity of the auditorium?

> Restate the problem: 90% of what number is 558?
> Write an equation: $0.9n = 558$
> Solve: $n = \frac{558}{.9}$
>
> $n = 620$

The capacity of the auditorium is 620 people.

<u>Example:</u> Shoes cost $42.00. Sales tax is 6%. What is the total cost of the shoes including tax?

Restate the problem: What is 6% of $42.00?
Write an equation: $n = 0.06 \times \$42.00$
Solve: $n = \$2.52$

Add the sales tax to the cost. $42.00 + $2.52 = $44.52
The total cost of the shoes, including sales tax, is $44.52.

An alternative method would be to multiply $42.00 by 1.06.
$42.00 x 1.06 = $44.52 (cost including sales tax)

Common Equivalents

$\dfrac{1}{2} = 0.5 = 50\%$

$\dfrac{1}{3} = 0.333 = 33\dfrac{1}{3}\%$

$\dfrac{1}{4} = 0.25 = 25\%$

$\dfrac{1}{5} = 0.2 = 20\%$

$\dfrac{1}{6} = 0.1667 = 16\dfrac{2}{3}\%$

$\dfrac{1}{8} = 0.125 = 12\dfrac{1}{2}\%$

$\dfrac{1}{10} = 0.1 = 10\%$

$\dfrac{2}{3} = 0.6667 = 66\dfrac{2}{3}\%$

$\dfrac{5}{6} = 0.833 = 83\dfrac{1}{3}\%$

$\dfrac{3}{8} = 0.375 = 37\dfrac{1}{2}\%$

$\dfrac{5}{8} = 0.625 = 62\dfrac{1}{2}\%$

$\dfrac{7}{8} = 0.875 = 87\dfrac{1}{2}\%$

$1 = 1.0 = 100\%$

COMPETENCY 6   **KNOWLEDGE OF FOUNDATIONS OF ALGEBRA**

Skill 6.1   Predict missing or subsequent terms in numerical, algebraic, and pictorial patterns

The most common **numerical patterns** are arithmetic sequences and geometric sequences. In an arithmetic sequence, each term is separated from the next by a fixed number (e.g. 3,6,9,12,15...). In a geometric sequence, each term in the series is multiplied by a fixed number to get the next term (e.g. 3, 6,12,24,48...).

An **arithmetic sequence** is a set of numbers with a common difference between the terms. Terms and the distance between terms can be calculated using use the following formula:

$$a_n = a_1 + (n-1)d \text{ where}$$

a_1 = the first term
a_n = the nth term (general term)
n = the number of the term in the sequence
d = the common difference

The formula essentially expresses the arithmetic sequence as an **algebraic pattern** $a_1, a_1+d, a_1+2d, a_1+3d...$ And so on where any numbers can be substituted for a_1 and d to derive different numerical sequences.

Example: Find the 8th term of the arithmetic sequence 5, 8, 11, 14...

$a_n = a_1 + (n-1)d$
$a_1 = 5$ identify the 1st term
$d = 8 - 5 = 3$ find d
$a_8 = 5 + (8-1)3$ substitute
$a_8 = 26$

Example: Given two terms of an arithmetic sequence, find a_1 and d

$a_4 = 21$ $a_6 = 32$
$a_n = a_1 + (n-1)d$ $a_4 = 21, n = 4$
$21 = a_1 + (4-1)d$ $a_6 = 32, n = 6$
$32 = a_1 + (6-1)d$

$21 = a_1 + 3d$ solve the system of equations
$32 = a_1 + 5d$

$32 = a_1 + 5d$
$\underline{-21 = -a_1 - 3d}$ multiply by -1
$11 = 2d$ add the equations
$5.5 = d$

$$21 = a_1 + 3(5.5)$$ substitute d = 5.5 into either equation
$$21 = a_1 + 16.5$$
$$a_1 = 4.5$$

The sequence begins with 4.5 and has a common difference of 5.5 between numbers.

A **geometric sequence** is a series of numbers in which a common ratio can be multiplied by a term to yield the next term. The common ratio can be calculated using the formula:

$$r = \frac{a_{n+1}}{a_n} \text{ where } \quad r = \text{common ratio}$$
$$a_n = \text{the nth term}$$

The ratio is then used in the geometric sequence formula: $a_n = a_1 r^{n-1}$

The formula essentially expresses the geometric sequence as an **algebraic pattern** $a_1, a_1r, a_1r^2, a_1r^3, a_1r^4\ldots.$ and so on where any numbers can be substituted for a_1 and r to derive different numerical sequences.

Example: Find the 8th term of the geometric sequence 2, 8, 32, 128...

$$r = \frac{a_{n+1}}{a_n}$$ use common ratio formula to find ratio

$$r = \frac{8}{2}$$ substitute $a_n = 2$, $a_{n+1} = 8$
$$r = 4$$

$$a_n = a_1 \cdot r^{n-1}$$ use r = 4 to solve for the 8th term
$$a_8 = 2 \cdot 4^{8-1}$$
$$a_8 = 32,768$$

Even though arithmetic and geometric sequences are the most common patterns, one can have series based on other rules as well. In some problems, the student will not be given the rule that governs a pattern but will have to inspect the pattern to find out what the rule is.

Example: Find the next term in the series 1, 1, 2, 3, 5, 8...

Inspecting the terms in the series, one finds that this pattern is neither arithmetic nor geometric. Every term in the series is a sum of the previous two terms. Thus, the next term = 5+8 =13. This particular sequence is a well-known series named the Fibonacci sequence.

Just like the arithmetic and geometric sequences discussed before, other patterns can be created using algebraic variables. Patterns may also be pictorial. In each case, one can predict subsequent terms or find a missing term by first discovering the rule that governs the pattern.

Example: Find the next term in the sequence $ax^2y, ax^4y^2, ax^6y^3, \ldots$

Inspecting the pattern, we see that this is a geometric sequence with common ratio x^2y. Thus, the next term = $ax^6y^3 \times x^2y = ax^8y^4$.

Example: Find the next term in the pattern:

Inspecting the pattern, one observes that it has alternating squares and circles that include a number of hearts that increases by two for each subsequent term.

Hence, the next term in the pattern will be as follows:

Skill 6.2   Analyze relationships between tables, graphs, or rules.

A relationship between two quantities can be shown using a table, graph or rule.

Example: A pair of sunglasses sells for $9. The relationship between the total amount earned, y, and the total number of $9 sunglasses sold, x, can be shown using the following.

A rule: y = $9x

A table using this data would appear as:

number of sunglasses sold	1	5	10	15
total dollars earned($)	9	45	90	135

Each *(x, y)* relationship between a pair of values is called the coordinate pair and can be plotted on a graph. The coordinate pairs *(1, 9)*, *(5, 45)*, *(10, 90)*, and *(15, 135)*, are plotted on the graph below.

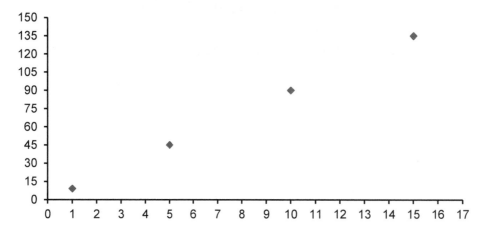

The graph above shows a linear relationship. A linear relationship is one in which two quantities are proportional to each other. Doubling *x* also doubles *y*. On a graph, a straight line that passes through the origin depicts a linear relationship.

Another type of relationship is a nonlinear relationship. This is one in which change in one quantity does not affect the other quantity to the same extent. A nonlinear graph, such as the graph below, has a curved line.

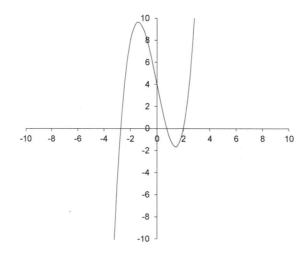

Additionally, it is helpful to recognize whether a certain relationship or pairing represents a function or not. While any pairing is a relation, only certain relations qualify as functions.

By definition, A **RELATION** is any set of ordered pairs, with the **DOMAIN OF A RELATION** being the set consisting of all the first coordinates of the ordered pairs, and the **RANGE OF A RELATION** being the set consisting of all the second coordinates of the ordered pairs. A **MAPPING** is a diagram with arrows drawn from each element of the domain to the corresponding elements of the range. If two arrows are drawn from the same element of the domain, then the mapping does not represent a function.

More specifically, a **FUNCTION** is a relation in which all ordered pairs have different first coordinates. (No x values are repeated.)

Example: Determine the domain and range of this mapping.

domain: {4, –5}

range: {6, 8, 11 }

This mapping does NOT represent a function, since the domain value of -5 is matched with two different range values.

When a graph is used to show a relation, the **vertical line test** can be used to determine whether the graph represents a function or not. If any vertical line intersects the graph of a relation in more than one point, then the relation is not a function.

Skill 6.3   Simplify rational and irrational expressions

A **rational expression** or a rational algebraic expression is the quotient of two polynomials. The divisor can <u>never</u> be zero.

A rational expression is in **simplest form** when the numerator and denominator have no common factor except for 1 or –1. To simplify a rational expression, factor the numerator and denominator completely, and then divide by their common factors.

Example: Simplify $\dfrac{4x^3 - 4x^2 + x}{4x^3 - x}$

$$\dfrac{x(4x^2 - 4x + 1)}{x(4x^2 - 1)}$$

$$\dfrac{x(2x - 1)(2x - 1)}{x(2x - 1)(2x + 1)}$$ Divide the numerator and denominator by $x(2x - 1)$

$$\dfrac{2x - 1}{2x + 1}$$

To reduce a rational expression with more than one term in the denominator, the expression must be factored first. Factors that are exactly the same will cancel and each becomes 1. Factors that have exactly the opposite signs of each other, such as (a – b) and (b – a), will cancel; one factor becomes 1 and the other becomes -1.

Example: Simplify

$$\frac{24x^3y^6z^3}{8x^2y^2z} = 3xy^4z^2$$

Example: Simplify

$$\frac{3x^2 - 14xy - 5y^2}{x^2 - 25y^2} = \frac{(3x + y)(x - 5y)}{(x + 5y)(x - 5y)} = \frac{3x + y}{x + 5y}$$

Irrational or radical expressions are simplified by minimizing the use of the radical as far as possible; i.e. removing whatever numbers and variables can be removed from under the radical sign. To simplify a radical, follow these steps:

1) Find the prime factorization of the number or coefficient.
2) For **square roots**, group like factors in pairs. For cube roots, arrange like factors in groups of three. For n^{th} roots, group like factors in groups of n.
3) For each of these groups, put one of the factors outside the radical. Any factors that cannot be combined in groups should be multiplied together and left inside the radical.

The index number of a radical is the little number on the front of the radical. For a cube root, the index is 3. If no index appears, then the index is 2 and is the square root.

Example: Simplify $\sqrt[3]{432}$

$$\sqrt[3]{432} = \sqrt[3]{3 \times 2 \times 2 \times 2 \times 3 \times 3 \times 2} = \sqrt[3]{3^3 2^4} = 3 \cdot 2 \cdot \sqrt[3]{2} = 6 \cdot \sqrt[3]{2}$$

Example: $\sqrt{50a^4b^7} = \sqrt{5 \cdot 5 \cdot 2 \cdot a^4 \cdot b^7} = 5a^2b^3\sqrt{2b}$

Note: Remember that the square root of a negative number can be designated by replacing the negative sign inside that square root with an "*i*" in front of the radical (to signify an imaginary number). Then simplify the remaining positive radical by the normal method. Include the *i* outside the radical as a part of the answer.

If the index number is an odd number, you can still simplify the radical to get a negative solution.

While adding and subtracting expressions involving radicals, like radicals can be combined.

Example: Simplify $\sqrt{288} + \sqrt{50} + \sqrt{12}$

$$\sqrt{288} + \sqrt{50} + \sqrt{12} = \sqrt{2 \times 144} + \sqrt{25 \times 2} + \sqrt{4 \times 3}$$
$$= 12\sqrt{2} + 5\sqrt{2} + 2\sqrt{3} = 17\sqrt{2} + 2\sqrt{3}$$

When there is a binomial radical expression in the denominator, remove the radical from the denominator by multiplying both the numerator and the denominator by the conjugate (sign between terms reversed) of the radical expression.

Example: Simplify $\dfrac{4}{3 + \sqrt{5}}$

$$\frac{4}{3 + \sqrt{5}} = \frac{4(3 - \sqrt{5})}{(3 + \sqrt{5})(3 - \sqrt{5})} = \frac{4(3 - \sqrt{5})}{9 - 5} = 3 - \sqrt{5}$$

Skill 6.4   Simplify expressions involving radicals and rational exponents using the properties of exponents

A radical is an integral root of a real number. The nth root of a real number a is written as $\sqrt[n]{a}$ where n is a positive integer greater than 1. Familiar radicals include square roots (e.g. $\sqrt{6}$, the number 2 is not written with the root symbol by convention) and cube roots (e.g. $\sqrt[3]{5}$).

A radical is expressed using a rational exponent in the following way: $\sqrt[n]{a} = a^{\frac{1}{n}}$

Example: $\sqrt{5} = 5^{\frac{1}{2}}$; $\sqrt[5]{7} = 7^{\frac{1}{5}}$

The exponent laws and properties discussed in Skill 7.9 can be applied to simplify expressions with rational exponents as well.

Example: $(\sqrt[5]{6})^3 = (6^{\frac{1}{5}})^3 = 6^{\frac{1}{5} \times 3} = 6^{\frac{3}{5}}$

Example: $\sqrt[3]{27a^{15}} = (27a^{15})^{\frac{1}{3}} = 27^{\frac{1}{3}}(a^{15})^{\frac{1}{3}} = 3a^5$

Example: $\dfrac{\sqrt{x}}{\sqrt[3]{x}} = \dfrac{x^{\frac{1}{2}}}{x^{\frac{1}{3}}} = x^{\frac{1}{2} - \frac{1}{3}} = x^{\frac{3-2}{6}} = x^{\frac{1}{6}} = \sqrt[6]{x}$

Example: We can use rational exponents to demonstrate taking the product 5 times of $\sqrt[5]{7}$ is 7.

$$\sqrt[5]{7} \times \sqrt[5]{7} \times \sqrt[5]{7} \times \sqrt[5]{7} \times \sqrt[5]{7} = 7^{\frac{1}{5}} \times 7^{\frac{1}{5}} \times 7^{\frac{1}{5}} \times 7^{\frac{1}{5}} \times 7^{\frac{1}{5}} = 7^{\frac{1}{5}+\frac{1}{5}+\frac{1}{5}+\frac{1}{5}+\frac{1}{5}} = 7^{\frac{5}{5}} = 7$$

Alternatively,

$$(\sqrt[5]{7})^5 = (7^{\frac{1}{5}})^5 = 7^{\frac{1}{5} \times 5} = 7$$

Skill 6.5 Solve equations or inequalities with one variable, including absolute values

A **linear equation with one variable** can be written in the form **ax + b = 0**, where a and b are real numbers and $a \neq 0$.

An equation can be solved by performing the same operations on both sides of the equation.

Example: Solve $4x - 3 = -5x + 6$ for x.

$4x - 3 = -5x + 6$	
$(4x - 3) + 3 = (-5x + 6) + 3$	Add 3.
$4x = {}^-5x + 9$	Simplify.
$4x + 5x = ({}^-5x + 9) + 5x$	Add 5x.
$\dfrac{9x}{9} = \dfrac{9}{9}$	Divide by 9.
$x = 1$	Simplify.

To **check**, substitute the solution into the original equation.

$$4x - 3 = -5x + 6$$
$$4(1) - 3 \ ? -5(1) + 6$$
$$1 = 1$$

An **inequality** is a statement that two expressions are *not* equal. The symbols used are $<$ (less than), $>$ (greater than), $\leq$ (less than or equal to), $\geq$ (greater than or equal to), and $\neq$ (not equal to). Many inequalities have an infinite number of solutions. Methods for solving inequalities are similar to those used for solving equations. However, **when both sides of an inequality are multiplied or divided by a negative real number, the inequality sign is reversed.**

Example: Solve $3x - 2 > 13$ for x.

$$(3x - 2) + 2 > 13 + 2 \qquad \text{Add 2.}$$
$$\frac{3x}{3} > \frac{15}{3} \qquad \text{Divide by 3.}$$
$$x > 5 \qquad \text{Simplify.}$$

Thus, the solution set is all real numbers greater than 5.

Example: Solve $x + 11 > 5x + 3$ for x.

$$(x + 11) - 11 > (5x + 3) - 11 \qquad \text{Subtract 11.}$$
$$x > 5x - 8 \qquad \text{Simplify.}$$
$$x - 5x > 5x - 8 - 5x \qquad \text{Subtract 5x.}$$
$$-4x > -8 \qquad \text{Simplify.}$$
$$x < 2$$

Divide by –4 and Reverse the inequality sign.
Thus, the solution set is all real numbers less than 2.

The **absolute value** of a real number is the distance that number is from 0 on a number line. Because distances are always positive, the absolute value will also always be the positive.

$$|x| = x \text{ when } x \geq 0 \text{ and}$$
$$|x| = -x \text{ when } x < 0.$$

Note the negative sign in front of the x when $x < 0$. In this case, the negative should be thought of as opposite. Therefore, the opposite of a negative number is a positive number (i.e. $|-5| = -(-5) = 5$).

Example: Find the absolute value of 7.
$$|7| = 7$$

Example: Find the absolute value of -13.
$$|-13| = -(-13) = 13$$

To solve linear equations with absolute value, derive two equations.
If $|x| = n$, then $x = n$ or $x = -n$

Example: Find the values of y that satisfy $|y - 7| = 2$.

$$y - 7 = 2 \quad or \quad y - 7 = -2$$
$$y = 9 \qquad or \qquad y = 5$$

The solutions must be checked.

$|y - 7| = 2$	$|y - 7| = 2$
$|9 - 7| = 2$	$|5 - 7| = 2$
$|2| = 2$	$|-2| = 2$
$2 = 2$	$2 = 2$
true	true

Example: Find the values of x that satisfy $|3x| + 4 = x$.

$$|3x| + 4 = x$$
$$|3x| = x - 4$$
$$3x = x - 4 \quad or \quad 3x = -(x - 4)$$
$$2x = -4 \qquad\qquad 3x = -x + 4$$
$$\qquad\qquad\qquad\qquad 4x = 4$$
$$x = -2 \quad or \quad x = 1$$

The solutions must be checked.

$|3x| + 4 = -2$	$|3x| + 4 = -2$
$|3(-2)| + 4 = -2$	$|3(1)| + 4 = -2$
$|-6| + 4 = -2$	$|3| + 4 = -2$
$6 + 4 = -2$	$3 + 4 = -2$
$10 \neq -2$	$7 \neq -2$

Since no solution is true, the solution set is empty.

An **inequality with absolute value** can be solved in a similar manner to an equation, for $r > 0$ (where r is a positive real number).

1) if $|x| < r$ then $x < r$ and $x > -r$ (alternate form: $-r < x < r$)
2) if $|x| > r$ then $x < -r$ or $x > r$

<u>Example</u>: Find the values of x that satisfy $|x - 1| < 4$.

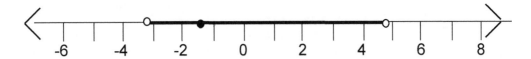

$$x - 1 < 4 \quad \text{and} \quad x - 1 > -4$$
$$x < 5 \quad \text{and} \quad x > -3 \text{ (alternate form: } -3 < x < 5)$$

Thus, the solution set is all real numbers between -3 and 5.

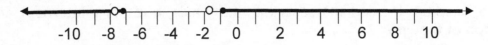

To **check**, choose a random value in the solution set.

If $x = -1$ then
$$|x - 1| < 4$$
$$|-1 - 1| < 4$$
$$|-2| < 4 \quad < 4$$
$$2 < 4$$
True

<u>Example</u>: Find the values of x that satisfy $|4 + x| - 3 \geq 0$.

$$|4 + x| - 3 \geq 0$$
$$|4 + x| \geq 3$$

$$4 + x \leq -3 \text{ OR } 4 + x \geq 3$$
$$x \leq -7 \text{ OR } x \geq -1$$

The solution set is all real number less than -7 or greater than -1.

To check, choose two random values in the solution set.
Try $x = 4$ and $x = -9$

$$|4 + 4| - 3 \geq 0, \quad |4 + (-9)| - 3 \geq 0$$
$$|8| - 3 \geq 0, \quad |-5| - 3 \geq 0$$
$$5 \geq 0 \quad \quad 2 \geq 0$$
True \quad\quad\quad True

Skill 6.6 **Identify graphs of inequalities involving one variable on a number line**

When graphing a linear inequality, the dot on the number line will be hollow if the inequality sign is < or > and solid if the inequality sign is ≥ or ≤. The arrow goes to the right for ≥ or > and to the left for ≤ or <.

Example: Solve 2(3x-7)>10x-2 for x.

$$2(3x-7) > 10x-2$$
$$6x-14 > 10x-2$$
$$-4x > 12$$
$$x < -3$$

Note the change of inequality symbol when dividing by a negative.

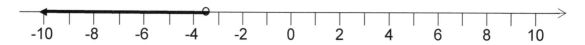

Skill 6.7 **Identify graphs of linear equations or inequalities involving two variables on the coordinate plane**

First-degree equations have exponents no greater than one and are also known as **linear equations** because their graph is a line.

To graph a first- degree equation, find both one point on the line and the slope of the line. The best way to find a point and the slope is to solve the equation for y. A linear equation that has been solved for y is in **slope-intercept form, y=mx+b**. The point (0,**b**) is where the line intersects with the y-axis, **b is the y-intercept** and **m is the slope of the line**.

Another way to graph a linear equation is to find any two points on the line and connect them. To find points on the line, substitute any number for x, solve for y, then repeat with another number for x. Often the two easiest points to find are the intercepts. To find the intercepts, substitute 0 for x and solve for y, then substitute 0 for y and solve for x. Note that this method will only work when the slope is a nonzero and defined. It will not work for vertical and horizontal lines as defined below.

If the equation solves to **x = any number**, the graph is a **vertical line**. It only has an x intercept, and its slope is **undefined**.

If the equation solves to **y = any number**, the graph is a **horizontal line**. It only has a y intercept, and its slope is **0 (zero)**.

Lines will go up and to the right when the slope (m) is positive. Lines with negative slopes (m) will go down as they go to the right.

When graphing a **linear inequality**, the method of determining the path of the line is the same. However, the line will be dotted if the inequality sign is < or >. If the inequality signs are either ≥ or ≤ , the line on the graph will be solid. Shade above the line when the inequality sign is ≥ or >. Shade below the line when the inequality sign is < or≤. For inequalities of the form x>,x²,x<, or x³ a given number, draw a vertical line (solid or dotted). Shade to the right for > or≥. Shade to the left for < or ≤. **Remember: Dividing or multiplying by a negative number will reverse the direction of the inequality sign.**

In the examples shown below, the equation or inequality has first been expressed in slope-intercept form.

In the graph shown on the left, the slope of the straight line is -5/2 (the line goes down from left to right due to the negative slope) and the y-intercept of the straight line is 3.

In the graph shown on the right, the straight line has a positive slope 3/2 and a y-intercept of -3. Since this is an inequality, the solution is represented by a whole shaded area instead of a single line. The graph reflects the fact that the values of y are less than (shading below line) or equal to (solid line) the right hand side.

$$5x+2y=6$$
$$y=\frac{-5}{2}x+3$$

$$3x-2y \geq 6$$
$$y \leq \frac{3}{2}x-3$$

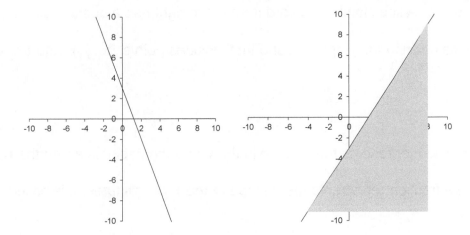

An example of a graph with only an x-intercept is given below.

$$3x+12<-3$$

$$x<-5$$

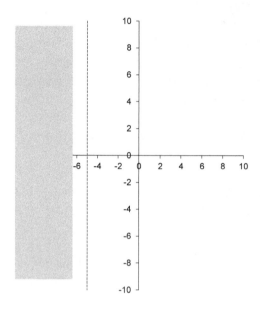

Skill 6.8   Identify the interpretation of slope and intercepts, given a real world context

The **slope** of a line is the "slant" of the line. A line slanting downward from left to right has a negative slope. A line slanting upward from left to right has a positive slope.

The formula for calculating the slope of a line that includes points (x_1, y_1) and (x_2, y_2) is:

$$\text{slope} = \frac{y_2 - y_1}{x_2 - x_1}$$

The top of the fraction represents the change in the **y**-coordinates; it is called the **rise**.

The bottom of the fraction represents the change in the **x**-coordinates; it is called the **run.**

Example: Find the slope of a line with points at (2, 2) and (7, 8).

$$\frac{(8)-(2)}{(7)-(2)}$$ plug the values into the formula

$$\frac{6}{5}$$ solve the rise over run

$= 1.2$ solve for the slope

A useful application for slope involves the concept of rate of change, or how fast a value is increasing or decreasing. Some examples of rates of change are "miles per hour," "gallons of water per day," and "dollars per year."

Example: The town of Verdant Slopes has been experiencing a boom in population growth. By the year 2000, the population had grown to 45,000, and by 2005, the population had reached 60,000.

Using the formula for slope as a model, find the average rate of change in population growth, expressing your answer in people per year. Then using the average rate of change determined, predict the population of Verdant Slopes in the year 2010.

Let t represent the time and p represent population growth. The two observances are represented by (t_1, p_1) and (t_2, p_2).

1st observance = (t_1, p_1) = (2000, 45000)
2nd observance = (t_2, p_2) = (2005, 60000)

Use the formula for slope to find the average rate of change.

$$\text{Rate of change} = \frac{p_2 - p_1}{t_2 - t_1}$$

$$= \frac{60000 - 45000}{2005 - 2000}$$

$$= \frac{15000}{5} = 3000 \, people / year$$

The average rate of change in population growth for Verdant Slopes between the years 2000 and 2005 was 3000 people/year.

The population of Verdant Slopes can be predicted using the following:
    3000 *people/year x 5 years = 15,000 people*
    60000 *people + 15000 people = 75,000 people*

At a continuing average rate of growth of 3000 people/year, the population of Verdant Slopes could be expected to reach 75,000 by the year 2010.

A natural extension of interpreting data through rate of change, or slope is to fully analyze its linear relationship, by investigating a linear equation representing the data. The equation of a straight line can be written in slope-intercept form, $y = mx + b$, where m is the slope and b is the y-intercept. The y-intercept is the y-coordinate of the point where a line crosses the y-axis. If the linear equation is in another form, one can rewrite the equation into slope intercept form, by algebraically rearranging terms as necessary. Once you find y=mx+b, you will know the slope is m and the y intercept is the value of b.

Alternatively, to find the y-intercept in any linear equation, substitute 0 for x and solve for y. This is the y-intercept.

The x-intercept is the x-coordinate of the point where a line crosses the x-axis. To find the x-intercept, substitute 0 for y and solve for x.

Example: Find the slope and intercepts of 3x+2y=14.

$$3x+2y=14$$
$$2y=-3x+14$$
$$y=\frac{-3}{2}x+7$$

The slope of the line is $\frac{-3}{2}$, the value of m.

The y-coordinate of the y-intercept of the line is 7, the value of b.

The intercepts can also be found using the original equation by substituting 0 for x and solving for y and substituting 0 for y and solving for x.

To find the y-intercept, let x = 0:

$$3(0) + 2y = 14$$
$$0 + 2y = 14$$
$$2y = 14$$
$$y = 7$$

(0, 7) is the y-intercept.

To find the x-intercept: let y = 0:

$$3x + 2(0) = 14$$
$$3x + 0 = 14$$
$$3x = 14$$
$$x = \frac{14}{3}$$

$(\frac{14}{3}, 0)$ is the x-intercept.

<u>Example:</u> Sketch the graph of the line represented by $2x + 3y = 6$.

Let $x = 0 \rightarrow 2(0) + 3y = 6$
$\rightarrow 3y = 6$
$\rightarrow y = 2$
$\rightarrow (0,2)$ is the y- intercept.

Let $y = 0 \rightarrow 2x + 3(0) = 6$
$\rightarrow 2x = 6$
$\rightarrow x = 3$
$\rightarrow (3,0)$ is the x-intercept.

Let $x = 1 \rightarrow 2(1) + 3y = 6$
$\rightarrow 2 + 3y = 6$
$\rightarrow 3y = 4$
$\rightarrow y = \dfrac{4}{3}$
$\rightarrow \left(1, \dfrac{4}{3}\right)$ is the third point.

Plotting the three points on the coordinate system, we get the following:

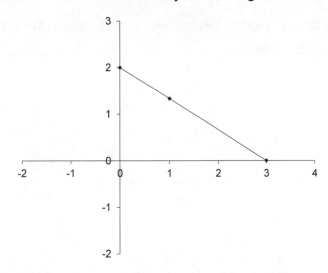

The slope of the line can be found using any two of the points:

$$m = \dfrac{2-0}{0-3} = -\dfrac{2}{3}$$

Many real world situations involve linear relationships, and often mirror the y=mx+b pattern. One example is the relationship between distance and time traveled when a car is moving at a constant speed. The relationship between the price and quantity of a bulk item bought at a store is also linear assuming that the unit price remains constant. These relationships can be expressed using the equation of a straight line and the slope is often used to describe a constant or average rate of change. These problems usually involve units of measure such as miles per hour or dollars per year. Where the line intercepts the x- and y- axis indicates a starting point or a point at which values change from positive to negative or negative to positive.

Example: A man drives a car at a speed of 30 mph along a straight road. Express the distance d traveled by the man as a function of the time t assuming the man's initial position is d_0.

The equation relating d and t is given by:

$$d = 30t + d_0$$

Notice that this equation is in the familiar slope-intercept form $y = mx + b$. In this case, time t (in hours) is the independent variable, the distance d (in miles) is the dependent variable. The **slope** is the **rate of change** of distance with time, i.e. the speed (in mph). The **y-intercept** or intercept on the distance axis d_0 represents the **initial position** of the car at the start time t=0.

The above equation is plotted below with d_0 =15 miles (the point on the graph where the line crosses the y-axis).

$$d = 30t + 15$$

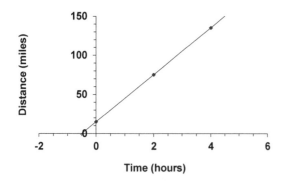

The **x-intercept** or intercept on the time axis represents the time at which the car would have been at d=0 assuming it was traveling with the same speed before t=0.

This value can be found by setting d=0 in the equation:

$$0 = 30t + 15$$
$$30t = -15$$
$$t = \frac{-15}{30} = -\frac{1}{2}hr$$

This simply means that if the car was at d=15 miles when we started measuring the time (t=0), it was at d=0 miles half an hour before that.

Skill 6.9   Determine an equation of a line.

The equation of a line can be found from its graph by finding its slope and y-intercept and substituting them in the slope-intercept form $y = mx + b$ (m is the slope, b is the y-intercept). For a detailed description of slope, intercepts and the slope-intercept form of a linear equation see **Skill 6.8**.

An alternate form of a linear equation is the point-slope form given below. Given the slope of a line and any one point (x_a, y_a) the line passes through, its equation may be written as $y - y_a = m(x - x_a)$

Example: Find the equation of a line that has a slope of -1.5 and passes through the point (3, 2).

Substituting the values of the slope m and the point (x_a, y_a) in the point-slope form of the equation we get

$$y - 2 = -1.5(x - 3) \text{ (point-slope form)}$$

Rearranging the terms,

$$y = -1.5 x + 6.5 \text{ (slope-intercept form)}$$

or, multiplying by 2 and moving the x-term to the left hand side,

$$3x + 2y = 13 \text{ (standard form)}$$

The equation of a line may be expressed in any one of the above forms. All of them are equally valid.

Example: Find the equation of a line through $(9, -6)$ and $(-1, 2)$.

$$\text{slope} = \frac{y_2 - y_1}{x_2 - x_1} = \frac{2 - (-6)}{-1 - 9} = \frac{8}{-10} = -\frac{4}{5}$$

$$y - y_a = m(x - x_a) \rightarrow y - 2 = -4/5(x - (-1)) \rightarrow$$
$$y - 2 = -4/5(x + 1) \rightarrow y - 2 = -4/5\, x - 4/5 \rightarrow$$
$$y = -4/5\, x + 6/5 \quad \text{Slope-intercept form.}$$

Multiplying by 5 to eliminate fractions, it is:

$$5y = -4x + 6 \rightarrow 4x + 5y = 6 \quad \text{Standard form.}$$

Skill 6.10   Find and estimate square roots

When finding the value of a square root, it is helpful to be familiar with the perfect squares, as they can be answered instantly. For instance:

$$\sqrt{81} = 9, \quad \sqrt{169} = 13 \text{ and } \sqrt{n^2} = n \text{ for } n \geq 0$$

The square root of a number that is not a perfect square is an irrational number, or a number that is represented by a non-terminating decimal. Therefore, there is no exact value to represent the square root. Often, it is appropriate to approximate the square root. This estimate can be found with a calculator or by hand through guessing and testing.

Example: By hand, estimate $\sqrt{75}$ to one place after the decimal.

The perfect squares on either side of 75 are $8^2 = 64$ and $9^2 = 81$. Since 75 is closer to 81, guess a value higher than 8.5, like 8.7. Then find $8.7^2 = 75.69$. Next, find $8.6^2 = 73.96$. Based on these values, 8.7 is the closer estimate for $\sqrt{75}$

Skill 6.11   Apply properties of operations (e.g., commutative, associative, distributive) to generate equivalent expressions

Real numbers exhibit the following addition and multiplication properties, where *a, b,* and *c* are real numbers. Multiplication is implied when there is no symbol between two variables. Thus, $a \times b$ can be written ab. Multiplication can also be indicated by a raised dot •.

Closure

The Closure Property for Whole-Number Addition states that the sum of any two whole numbers is a whole number.

Example: Since 2 and 5 are both whole numbers, 7 is also a whole number.

The Closure Property for Whole-Number Multiplication states that the product of any two whole numbers is a whole number.

Example: Since 3 and 4 are both whole numbers, 12 is also a whole number.

For any set of numbers to be closed under an operation, the result must be included within that set of numbers.

Commutative

The order of the addends or factors does not affect the sum or product.

$a + b = b + a$

Example: $5 + (-8) = (-8) + 5 = -3$

$ab = ba$

Example: $(-2) \times 6 = 6 \times (-2) = -12$

Associative

The grouping of the addends or factors does not affect the sum or product.

$(a + b) + c = a + (b + c)$

Example: $((-2) + 7) + 5 = (-2) + (7 + 5)$
$$5 + 5 = (-2) + 12$$
$$= 10$$

$(ab) c = a (bc)$

Example: $(3 \times (-7)) \times 5 = 3 \times ((-7) \times 5)$
$$(-21) \times 5 = 3 \times (-35)$$
$$= -105$$

Distributive

To multiply a sum by a number, multiply each addend by the number, then add the products.

$a(b + c) = ab + ac$

Example: $6 \times (-4 + 9) = (6 \times -4) + (6 \times 9)$
$6 \times 5 = -24 + 54 = 30$

Additive Identity (Property of Zero)

The sum of any number and zero is that number.

$a + 0 = a$

Example: $17 + 0 = 17$

Multiplicative Identity (Property of One)

The product of any number and one is that number.

$a \cdot 1 = a$

Example: $-34 \times 1 = -34$

Additive Inverse (Property of Opposites)

The sum of any number and its opposite is zero.

$a + (-a) = 0$

Example: $25 + -25 = 0$

Multiplicative Inverse (Property of Reciprocals)

The product of any number and its reciprocal is one.

$a \times \dfrac{1}{a} = 1$

Example: $5 \times \dfrac{1}{5} = 1$

Property of Denseness

Between any pair of rational numbers, there is at least one rational number. The set of natural numbers is not dense because between two consecutive natural numbers, there does not exist another natural number.

Example: Between 7.6 and 7.7, there is the rational number 7.65.
Between 3 and 4, there exists no other natural number.

Familiarity with these properties is essential to much of the simplification and solving work in Algebra. For instance, the Commutative Property aids in collecting like terms in an expression. $3x + 7y + 8 + 2y + 2$ can be changed to $3x + 7y + 2y + 8 + 2$ so that the like terms are adjacent. The expression then clearly simplifies to $3x + 9y + 10$.

The Additive Inverse and Additive Identity properties are used in the equation solving process. Consider the steps to solve $x+9 = 15$. The first step is to add -9 to both sides, as it is the additive inverse of 9. Then the resulting steps, $x + 9 + (-9) = 15 + (-9)$, or $x + 0 = 6$, $x = 6$ demonstrate the Additive Identity.

Furthermore, the Distributive Property helps in geometric applications, like conservation of area.

4	7
3	

11
3

$$3(4 + 7) \quad = \quad 3 (11)$$
$$12 + 21 \quad = \quad 33$$

While not every step of problem solving is always labeled with the Properties that have been used, students need to be aware of how and when the Properties are at work.

COMPETENCY 7   KNOWLEDGE OF ALGEBRAIC THINKING

Skill 7.1   Determine the impact when changing values of given linear and nonlinear functions. (e.g., change of y-intercept or coefficients)

The behavior of a function depends in large part on the parameters that define it. Function parameters are not to be confused with variables (or independent variables), which are a domain of values that can be input into the function to yield a range of resulting values. Consider the linear equation $y = mx + b$.

Recalling Skills 6.8 and 6.9, m represents the slope of the line and b is the y intercept. When m is a positive number, the line will rise to the right; but changing m to a negative number causes the line to fall to the right. Changing the value of b will raise or lower the spot where the line crosses the y- axis.

Another good example worthy of analysis is a quadratic equation: $y = ax^2 + bx + c$

The function y is expressed in terms of the variable x and the coefficients, or parameters a, b and c. Of particular interest is determining how variation of these parameters affects the function. To do this, one must look at the relationships between the parameters, the variables and the overall function.

Consider once again the case of the general quadratic function. One of the simplest ways to analyze the effect of changing parameters is to isolate particular terms of the function by setting certain parameters to zero (if allowed by the function—in some cases, such as where a parameter is a factor in the denominator of a fraction, this may not be possible because setting the parameter to zero causes the function to be undefined).

First, consider the case where b and c are equal to zero. This leaves the following expression for function y:

$$y = ax^2$$

Clearly, since x^2 is always positive (for real values of x), the product of a and x^2, along with the sign of a, determines the sign of y for any given x value. Also, since y is zero at $x = 0$, regardless of the value of a, it can then be seen that increasing (or decreasing) the magnitude of a causes the slope of the function to increase (decrease) at any given point $(x, y(x))$.

Example graphs of different values for *a* are shown below.

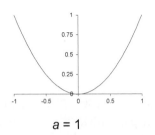

a = 1

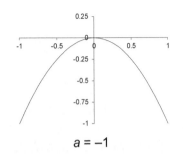

a = −1

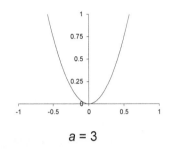

a = 3

A similar approach can be used for the other two parameters, *b* and *c*. By examining the effect on the function of varying these parameters independently, and then by looking at the relationship among the different parts, the behavior of the total function can be determined. In the case of the general quadratic function, then, the three terms (which can be examined independently) must ultimately be added. The result is a sum of the behaviors of the three terms; the value of *a* determines whether the function is concave up or concave down (along with the relative steepness of the slope at each point), the value of *b* determines (in part) the location of the plot of the function along the *x*- and *y*-axes, and the value of *c* contributes to the location of the function along the *y*-axis.

Another example function is the following:

$$y = a\ln(bx)$$

In this case, the parameters cannot be isolated simply by setting them equal to zero, but they can be isolated by setting them, in turn, equal to one. For instance, by setting *a* = 1, the behavior of the function ln (*bx*) can be examined to determine the effect of changing the parameter *b*. Likewise, by setting *b* = 1, the behavior of the function *a* ln *x* can be examined to determine the effect of changing the parameter *a*. Consider the following graphs for various *a* and *b* parameter values.

a = 1, *b* = 1

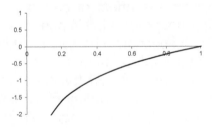

a = 1, *b* = 2

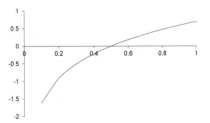

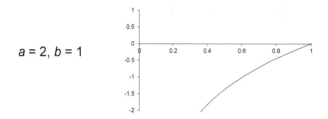

$a = 2,\ b = 1$

Certain changes in a function result in a translation of a graph, which means the graph is relocated on the coordinate plane. These changes in a given function, say y = f(x), can be summarized by the following adjustments:

1) y = f(x-h) moves the graph horizontally h units
2) y – k = f(x) moves the graph vertically ky units

<u>Example</u>: Move the graph of the function $y = x^2$ 2 units up and 4 units to the left.

To move the graph two units up, change y into y – 2. To move the graph 2 to the left, change x into x + 4. The new equation becomes (y – 2) = (x + 4)^2, or y = (x + 4)^2 + 2.

$$y = x^2 \qquad\qquad\qquad y = (x+4)^2 + 2$$

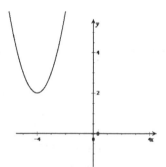

Although graphically viewing the effect of changing the parameters of a function is illustrative, sometimes it is not practical. It is possible, however, to determine the effect of varying parameters by inspection. The relationships between the parameters, the variables and the function itself determine the effects that result from changing those parameters. Sometimes the behavior of the function under changing parameters is clear, other times it is helpful to draw a rudimentary plot or simply calculate a few values of the function using several values for the variable or variables.

Skill 7.2   Identify the equation of a line that is perpendicular or parallel to a given line

Lines that are equidistant from each other and never intersect are **parallel**. Parallel lines, therefore, must have the same slope. Note that vertical lines are parallel to other vertical lines despite having undefined slopes.

Perpendicular lines form 90° angles at their intersection. The slopes of perpendicular lines are the negative reciprocals of each other. In other words, if a line has a slope of -2, a perpendicular line would have a slope of ½. Note that the product of these slopes is -1.

<u>Example:</u> One line passes through the points (–4, –6) and (4, 6); another line passes through the points (–5, –4) and (3, 8). Are these lines parallel, perpendicular or neither? Find the slopes.

$$m = \frac{y_2 - y_1}{x_2 - x_1}$$

$$m_1 = \frac{6 - (-6)}{4 - (-4)} = \frac{6 + 6}{4 + 4} = \frac{12}{8} = \frac{3}{2}$$

$$m_2 = \frac{8 - (-4)}{3 - (-5)} = \frac{8 + 4}{3 + 5} = \frac{12}{8} = \frac{3}{2}$$

Since the slopes are equal, the lines are parallel.

<u>Example:</u> One line passes through the points (1, –3) and (0, –6); another line passes through the points (4, 1) and (–2, 3). Are these lines parallel, perpendicular or neither? Find the slopes.

$$m = \frac{y_2 - y_1}{x_2 - x_1}$$

$$m_1 = \frac{-6 - (-3)}{0 - 1} = \frac{-6 + 3}{-1} = \frac{-3}{-1} = 3$$

$$m_2 = \frac{3 - 1}{-2 - 4} = \frac{2}{-6} = -\frac{1}{3}$$

The slopes are negative reciprocals, so the lines are perpendicular.

Example: One line passes through the points (–2, 4) and (2, 5); another line passes through the points (–1, 0) and (5, 4). Are these lines parallel, perpendicular or neither?

Find the slopes:

$$m = \frac{y_2 - y_1}{x_2 - x_1}$$

$$m_1 = \frac{5 - 4}{2 - (-2)} = \frac{1}{2 + 2} = \frac{1}{4}$$

$$m_2 = \frac{4 - 0}{5 - (-1)} = \frac{4}{5 + 1} = \frac{4}{6} = \frac{2}{3}$$

Since the slopes are not equal, the lines are not parallel. Since they are not negative reciprocals, they are not perpendicular either. Therefore, the answer is "neither."

Example: The equation of a line is $x + 3y = 0$. Determine whether it is parallel or perpendicular to the following straight lines.

(a) $y - 3x = 5$ (b) $y + x - 5 = 0$ (c) $2x + 6y = 7$

Putting the given equation in the slope-intercept form, we get

$$x + 3y = 0$$
$$\Rightarrow 3y = -x$$
$$\Rightarrow y = -\frac{1}{3}x$$

Therefore, the slope of the given line is $-\frac{1}{3}$.

We can find the slopes of the lines (a), (b) and (c) to determine whether they are parallel or perpendicular to the given line.

(a)
$$y - 3x = 5$$
$$\Rightarrow y = 3x + 5$$

The slope of this line is 3, the negative reciprocal of $-\frac{1}{3}$. Thus, this line is perpendicular to the given line.

(b)
$$y + x - 5 = 0$$
$$\Rightarrow y = -x + 5$$

The slope of this line is -1. Therefore, it is neither parallel nor perpendicular to the given line.

$$2x + 6y = 7$$

$$\text{(c)} \Rightarrow 6y = -2x + 7$$

$$\Rightarrow y = -\frac{1}{3}x + \frac{7}{6}$$

The slope of this line is $-\frac{1}{3}$. Hence, it is parallel to the given line.

Skill 7.3   Apply operations to analyze polynomials (e.g., finding zeros, factoring, arithmetic operations)

Many expressions and equations in Algebra are made up of polynomials. *Poly*, implies many terms. More specifically, *monomials* represent one term, *binomials* have two terms and *trinomials* have three. Being able to manipulate and organize polynomials is essential to success with many other algebraic operations.

When **adding and subtracting polynomials**, the objective is to collect like terms and arrange them in descending order, with respect to degree. For example:

$$(5x^4 - 8x^2 + 4x + 3) - (2x^4 - 4x^3 + 6x - 10) \text{ becomes } (5-2)x^4 + 4x^3 - 8x^2 + (4-6)x + (3+10)$$

or

$$3x^4 + 4x^3 - 8x^2 - 2x + 13$$

Multiplying polynomials requires a bit more strategy. In the general sense, when multiplying one polynomial by another, each term of the first polynomial must be distributed through the second.

$$(A+B)(3A+4AB+5B) = \quad 3A^2 + 4A^2B + 5AB \; + \; 3AB + 4AB^2 + 5B^2$$
$$3A^2 + 4A^2B + \mathbf{8}AB + 4AB^2 + 5B^2$$

Multiplying binomials occurs with such frequency that it earns its own, named strategy, called the FOIL method, standing for the products of the First-Outer-Inner-Last pairs of terms.

Take, for example, $(x+4)(x-7) = \quad x^2 + (-7)x + 4x + (-28)$
$$\text{F} \qquad \text{O} \quad \text{I} \quad \text{L}$$

The process of **dividing polynomials** can be carried out by either of two algorithms: long division or synthetic division. Synthetic division is only used when the divisor is of the form (x-r).

Example: $(x^4 + 2x^3 - 16x^2 - 2x + 15) \div (x + 5)$

The long division process mirrors the algorithm for numeric long division.

Synthetic division attempts to streamline this process by showing the long division process without writing the variables. We can set up the synthetic division as shown below. Inside the division bar, we place the coefficients of the dividend, and outside the division bar, we write the solution, or root, ($x = -5$) that we get by setting the divisor, $x + 5$, equal to zero.

$$-5 \; \Big| \; 1 \quad 2 \quad -16 \quad -2 \quad 15$$

Next, we carry the first coefficient down below the horizontal bar; then we begin performing the algorithm for synthetic division. The first step is shown below, followed by the final result. With each progression, the number on the bottom is multiplied by the root, -5, placed in the next column for addition with the entry above.

i) $-5 \; \Big| \; 1 \quad 2 \quad -16 \quad -2 \quad 15$
$\underline{}$
$ 1$

ii) $-5 \; \Big| \; 1 \quad 2 \quad -16 \quad -2 \quad 15$
$ -5$
$\underline{}$
$ 1 \quad -3$

iii) $-5 \; \Big| \; 1 \quad 2 \quad -16 \quad -2 \quad 15$
$ -5 \quad 15$
$\underline{}$
$ 1 \quad -3 \quad -1$

iv) $-5 \; \Big| \; 1 \quad 2 \quad -16 \quad -2 \quad 15$
$ -5 \quad 15 \quad 5$
$\underline{}$
$ 1 \quad -3 \quad -1 \quad 3$

v) $-5 \; \Big| \; 1 \quad 2 \quad -16 \quad -2 \quad 15$
$ -5 \quad 15 \quad 5 \quad -15$
$\underline{}$
$ 1 \quad -3 \quad -1 \quad 3 \quad 0$

Using the results of the synthetic division as the coefficients of the variable terms, we can now write the resulting polynomial, which is the solution to the problem: $x^3 - 3x^2 - x + 3$. (The last coefficient, 0 in this case, represents the remainder)

Since there is no remainder to this division, -5 is a root, or zero, of the polynomial.
$x^4 + 2x^3 - 16x^2 - 2x + 15$

Factoring is another operation applied to polynomials. Factoring aids in the simplification of an expression or can be part of the equation solving process. There are multiple levels of complexity of factoring.

First, always factor out the **greatest common monomial factors** before factoring further. To find the greatest common factor (GCF) of the terms in a polynomial,

1. Find the GCF of the coefficients.
2. Find the smallest degree of each variable to be found in any term.
3. Multiply then together to find the GCF of the terms.

Example: Factor $36x^4y + 18x^3y^3 - 9x^2y^6$

First, find the GCF of the coefficients 36, 18 and 9.

Prime factorization of each coefficient: $36 = 2^2 \cdot 3^2$; $18 = 2 \cdot 3^2$; $9 = 3^2$
Thus, GCF of the coefficients = $3^2 = 9$.
The smallest degree of x = 2
The smallest degree of y = 1

Thus, the GCF of the terms in the expression = $9x^2y$.

Factoring it out we get, $36x^4y + 18x^3y^3 - 9x^2y^6 = 9x^2y(4x^2 + 2xy^2 - y^5)$

Example: Factor $25abx^2 + 15acx + 40ax^5$

GCF of the coefficients 25, 15 and 40 = 5.
The smallest degree of a = 1.
The smallest degree of b = 0.
The smallest degree of c = 0.
The smallest degree of x = 1.

Thus, the GCF of the terms in the polynomial = 5ax.

Factoring it out we get, $25abx^2 + 15acx + 40ax^5 = 5ax(5bx + 3c + 8x^4)$

Oftentimes, the factoring process can involve multiple steps. Taking out the GCF should always be the first step of factoring, if possible. The resulting polynomial factor then should be inspected to see if it qualifies for any additional factoring.

After factoring out any GCFs, proceed as follows:

1) If a binomial factor exists, check to see if it is the **difference of 2 perfect squares**. If both terms are perfect squares, then it factors this way:
$$a^2 - b^2 = (a - b)(a + b)$$

Example: Factor completely $4x^2 - 25y^2$

No GCF; this is the difference of perfect squares.
$$4x^2 - 25y^2 = (2x - 5y)(2x + 5y)$$

2) A binomial may also represent the **sum or difference of 2 perfect cubes**.
$$a^3 - b^3 = (a - b)(a^2 + ab + b^2)$$
$$a^3 + b^3 = (a + b)(a^2 - ab + b^2)$$

Example: Factor completely $x^3 - 8y^3$ and $64a^3 + 27b^3$

$$x^3 - 8y^3 = (x - 2y)(x^2 + 2xy + 4y^2) \qquad \leftarrow \text{difference}$$
$$64a^3 + 27b^3 = (4a + 3b)(16a^2 - 12ab + 9b^2) \quad \leftarrow \text{sum}$$

3) If a trinomial remains, it can be a **perfect square**.
$$(a + b)^2 = a^2 + 2ab + b^2$$
$$(a - b)^2 = a^2 - 2ab + b^2$$

Example: Factor completely $4x^2 + 12xy + 9y^2$.

$$4x^2 + 12xy + 9y^2$$
$$= (2x)^2 + 2 \cdot (2x)(3y) + (3y)^2$$
$$= (2x + 3y)^2$$

Example: Factor completely $50a^3b^2 - 60a^2b^4 + 18ab^6$

$$50a^3b^2 - 60a^2b^4 + 18ab^6$$
$$= 2ab^2(25a^2 - 30ab^2 + 9b^4) \Rightarrow \text{Factor out GCF}$$
$$= 2ab^2((5a)^2 - 2(5a)(3b^2) + (3b^2)^2)$$
$$= 2ab^2(5a - 3b^2)^2$$

4) Some other trinomials can be factored into 2 binomials (un-FOILing). Be sure the terms of the trinomial are in descending order of exponents (i.e. in the form $ax^2 + bx + c$). If the last (constant) term of the trinomial has a "+" sign, the signs in the two factors will be the same as the sign in front of the second term of the trinomial. If the sign of the last term of a trinomial is a "−," then there will be one "+" and one "−" in the two factors. The first term of the trinomial can be factored to equal the first terms of the two factors. The last term of the trinomial can be factored

to equal the last terms of the two factors. Work backwards to determine the correct factors to multiply together to get the correct center term.

One method is to express the middle term as a sum of two terms such that the coefficients of the two terms multiplied together equal the product of the coefficient of the first term and the last term; i.e., given a trinomial $ax^2 + bx + c$, b must be expressed as the sum of two factors of ac.

Example: Factor completely $6x^2 - 2x - 8$

GCF of 2; Try to factor into 2 binomials:
$$6x^2 - 2x - 8 = 2(3x^2 - x - 4)$$

In the trinomial $3x^2 - x - 4$, a =3, b=-1, c=-4.

Thus -1 must be expressed as the sum of two factors of -12.
Find factors of -12: -1 & 12; -2 & 5; -3 & 4 and so on.

We see that -1 = -4 + 3.
Thus, we can write the trinomial $3x^2 - x - 4$ as $3x^2 - 4x + 3x - 4$

Grouping the 4 resulting terms in pairs, we get:
$$3x^2 - 4x + 3x - 4 = x(3x - 4) + (3x - 4) = (x + 1)(3x - 4)$$

Thus $6x^2 - 2x - 8 = 2(x + 1)(3x - 4)$

The final polynomial operation to be considered here will be **finding the zeros**. This directive asks for the number for x that will give the polynomial a value, or y coordinate when graphing, of 0.

Consider, for instance, finding zeroes of the polynomial

$x^3 + 4x^2 - 25x - 100$	Factor the polynomial and set the factors equal to zero. If (x-r) is a factor, then r will be a zero.
$x^2(x + 4) - 25(x + 4)$	pulling out GCF in first and second halves of the polynomial
$(x + 4)(x^2 - 25)$	pulling out GCF (x+4)
$(x + 4)(x - 5)(x + 5)$	Difference of two squares

From these three factors, we can determine that the zeroes of the polynomial are {-4, 5,-5}

For more practice with finding zeroes, specifically in quadratic polynomials, see Skill 7.6.

Skill 7.4   Solve systems of linear equations involving two variables using graphing, substitution, or elimination

Word problems can sometimes be solved by using a system of two equations with two unknowns. The system can be solved using either the **addition-subtraction method** (also known as **elimination**) or **substitution**.

Example: Farmer Greenjeans bought 4 cows and 6 sheep for $1700. Mr. Ziffel bought 3 cows and 12 sheep for $2400. If all the cows were the same price and all the sheep were another price, find the price charged for a cow and for a sheep.

Let x = price of a cow
Let y = price of a sheep

Farmer Greenjeans' equation would be: $4x + 6y = 1700$
Mr. Ziffel's equation would be: $3x + 12y = 2400$

To solve by **addition-subtraction** or **elimination**:

Eliminate one variable to solve for the other.

Multiply the first equation by -2: $-2(4x + 6y = 1700)$
Keep the other equation the same: $(3x + 12y = 2400)$

$$-8x - 12y = -3400$$
$$\underline{3x + 12y = 2400} \quad \text{Add the equations.}$$
$$-5x \qquad = -1000$$

$x = 200 \leftarrow$ The price of a cow was $200.

Solving for y, $y = 150 \leftarrow$ The price of a sheep was $150.

To solve by **substitution**:

Solve one of the equations for a variable. (Try to make an equation without fractions if possible.) Substitute this expression into the second equation, and then solve the resulting equation for the value of the remaining variable.

$$4x + 6y = 1700$$
$$3x + 12y = 2400 \leftarrow \text{Solve this equation for } x.$$

It becomes $x = 800 - 4y$. Now substitute $800 - 4y$ in place of x in the OTHER equation. $4x + 6y = 1700$ now becomes:

$$4(800 - 4y) + 6y = 1700$$
$$3200 - 16y + 6y = 1700$$
$$3200 - 10y = 1700$$
$$-10y = -1500$$
$$y = 150, \text{ or } \$150 \text{ for a sheep.}$$

Substituting 150 back into an equation for y, find x.

$$4x + 6(150) = 1700$$
$$4x + 900 = 1700$$
$$4x = 800$$

$$x = 200, \text{ or } \$200 \text{ for a cow.}$$

Example: Mrs. Winters bought 4 dresses and 6 pairs of shoes for $340. Mrs. Summers bought 3 dresses and 8 pairs of shoes for $360. If all the dresses were the same price and all the shoes were the same price, find the price charged for a dress and for a pair of shoes.

Let x = price of a dress
Let y = price of a pair of shoes

Then Mrs. Winters' equation would be: $4x + 6y = 340$
Mrs. Summers' equation would be: $3x + 8y = 360$

Solve by addition-subtraction:

Multiply the first equation by 4: $4(4x + 6y = 340)$
Multiply the second equation by -3: $-3(3x + 8y = 360)$

The equations can now be added together to eliminate one variable and solve for the other.

$$16x + 24y = 1360$$
$$\underline{-9x - 24y = -1080}$$
$$7x = 280$$
$$x = 40 \leftarrow \text{the price of a dress was } \$40$$

Solving for y, $y = 30 \leftarrow$ the price of a pair of shoes was $30

<u>Example:</u> Aardvark Taxi charges $4 initially plus $1 for every mile traveled. Baboon Taxi charges $6 initially plus $.75 for every mile traveled. Determine the mileage at which it becomes cheaper to ride with Baboon Taxi than it is to ride Aardvark Taxi.

Aardvark Taxi's equation:	$y = 1x + 4$
Baboon Taxi's equation:	$y = .75x + 6$
Use substitution:	$.75x + 6 = x + 4$
Multiply both sides by 4:	$3x + 24 = 4x + 16$
Solve for x:	$8 = x$

This tells you that, at 8 miles, the total charge for the two companies is the same. If you compare the charge for 1 mile, Aardvark charges $5 and Baboon charges $6.75. Therefore, Aardvark Taxi is cheaper for distances up to 8 miles, but Baboon is cheaper for distances greater than 8 miles.

This problem can also be solved by graphing the 2 equations.

$$y = 1x + 4 \qquad\qquad y = .75x + 6$$

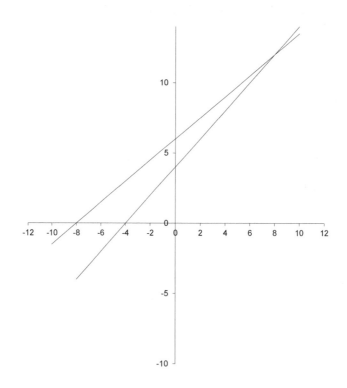

The lines intersect at (8, 12), therefore at 8 miles, both companies charge $12. For distances less than 8 miles, Aardvark Taxi charges less (the graph is below Baboon). For distances greater than 8 miles, Aardvark charges more (the graph is above Baboon).

Skill 7.5   Determine the solution set of a system of linear inequalities involving two variables

To graph an inequality, solve the inequality for y by changing the inequality to **slope intercept form**, $y < mx + b$. The point (0, b) is the y-intercept and m is the line's slope.

If the inequality solves to $x \geq$ **any number**, then the graph consists of a **vertical line**.

If the inequality solves to $y \leq$ **any number**, then the graph consists of a **horizontal line**.

When graphing a linear inequality, the line will be dotted if the inequality sign is < or > and solid if the inequality signs are either $\geq$ or $\leq$. Shade above the line when the inequality sign is $\geq$ or >. Shade below the line when the inequality sign is < or $\leq$. For inequalities of the forms $x >$ number, $x \leq$ number, $x <$ number, or $x \geq$ number, draw a vertical line (solid or dotted). Shade to the right for > or $\geq$.
Shade to the left for < or $\leq$.

Use these rules to graph and shade each inequality. The solution to a system of linear inequalities consists of the part of the graph where the solutions for both inequalities overlap. For instance, if the graph of one inequality is shaded with red and the graph of another inequality is shaded with blue, then the overlapping area would be shaded purple. The purple area would be the points in the solution set of this system.

Example: Solve by graphing:

$$x + y \leq 6$$
$$x - 2y \leq 6$$

Solving the inequalities for y, they become:

$$y \leq -x + 6 \quad (y\text{-intercept of 6 and slope} = -1)$$
$$y \geq 1/2 x - 3 \quad (y\text{- intercept of } -3 \text{ and slope} = 1/2)$$

A graph with the solution area shaded is shown below. It is the area where the solution to $y \le -x + 6$ (area below the line) overlaps with the solution to $y \ge 1/2x - 3$ (area above the line).

$x + y \le 6$

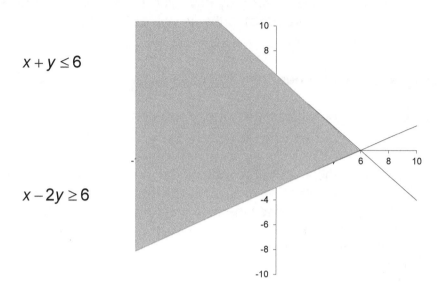

$x - 2y \ge 6$

Skill 7.6   Use quadratic equations to solve abstract and realistic problems

A **quadratic equation** is written in the form $ax^2 + bx + c = 0$. A quadratic equation is often solved by **factoring the quadratic expression** into two linear factors. Since at least one of the factors must be zero in order to satisfy the equation, the possible solutions to the quadratic equation are found by setting each factor, in turn, to zero.

<u>Example</u>: Solve for x.

$$x^2 + 10x - 24 = 0$$
$$(x + 12)(x - 2) = 0 \qquad \text{Factor.}$$
$$x + 12 = 0 \text{ or } x - 2 = 0 \qquad \text{Set each factor equal to 0.}$$
$$x = -12 \qquad x = 2 \qquad \text{Solve.}$$

Check:

$$x^2 + 10x - 24 = 0$$
$$(-12)^2 + 10(-12) - 24 = 0 \qquad (2)^2 + 10(2) - 24 = 0$$
$$144 - 120 - 24 = 0 \qquad 4 + 20 - 24 = 0$$
$$0 = 0 \qquad 0 = 0$$

An alternate method for solving a quadratic equation is **completing the square**. In order to complete the square, the coefficient of the x^2 term must be 1. Isolate the x^2 and x terms. Then add the half of the coefficient of the x term squared to both sides of the equation. Finally take the square root of both sides and solve for x.

<u>Example</u>: Solve for x.

$$x^2 - 6x + 8 = 0$$

$$x^2 - 6x = {}^{-}8 \qquad \text{Move the constant to the right side.}$$

$$x^2 - 6x + 9 = {}^{-}8 + 9 \qquad \text{Add the square of half the coefficient of } x \text{ to both sides.}$$

$$(x - 3)^2 = 1 \qquad \text{Write the left side as a perfect square.}$$

$$x - 3 = \pm\sqrt{1} \qquad \text{Take the square root of both sides.}$$

$$x - 3 = 1 \qquad x - 3 = {}^{-}1 \qquad \text{Solve.}$$

$$x = 4 \qquad x = 2$$

Check:

$$x^2 - 6x + 8 = 0$$

$$4^2 - 6(4) + 8 = 0 \qquad\qquad 2^2 - 6(2) + 8 = 0$$

$$16 - 24 + 8 = 0 \qquad\qquad 4 - 12 + 8 = 0$$

$$0 = 0 \qquad\qquad\qquad 0 = 0$$

A quadratic equation may also be solved using the **quadratic formula**. This is particularly useful in cases where the quadratic expression cannot be factored. The equation must be put in the form $ax^2 + bx + c = 0$. The solution is obtained by substituting the values of the coefficients a, b and c into the formula:

$$x = \frac{-b \pm \sqrt{b^2 - 4ac}}{2a}$$

Example: Solve the equation $3x^2=7+2x$ for x.

$$3x^2 = 7 + 2x \rightarrow 3x^2 - 2x - 7 = 0$$

$$a = 3 \quad b = -2 \quad c = -7$$

$$x = \frac{-(-2) \pm \sqrt{(-2)^2 - 4(3)(-7)}}{2(3)}$$

$$x = \frac{2 \pm \sqrt{4 + 84}}{6}$$

$$x = \frac{2 \pm \sqrt{88}}{6}$$

$$x = \frac{2 \pm 2\sqrt{22}}{6}$$

$$x = \frac{1 \pm \sqrt{22}}{3}$$

Some real-world problems, when expressed in terms of algebra, yield quadratic equations or inequalities. The techniques and strategies for solving quadratics can be used to tackle these problems.

Example: A family is planning to add a new room to their house. They would like the room to have a length that is 10 ft more than the width and a total area of 375 sq. feet. Find the length and width of the room.

Let x be the width of the room.
Length of the room = x+10

Thus,
$$x(x + 10) = 375$$
$$x^2 + 10x - 375 = 0$$

Factor the quadratic expression to solve the equation:

$x^2 + 25x - 15x - 375 = 0$ Break up the middle

$x(x + 25) - 15(x + 25) = 0$ term using factors of 375

$(x + 25)(x - 15) = 0$

$x = -25$ or $x = 15$

Since the dimension of a room cannot be negative, we choose the positive solution x=15.

Thus, the width of the room is 15 ft and the length of the room is 25ft.

<u>Example</u>: A family wants to enclose 3 sides of a rectangular garden with 200 feet of fence. A wall borders the fourth side of the garden. In order to have a garden with an area of **at least** 4800 square feet, find the dimensions the garden should be.

Existing Wall Solution:
Let $x =$ distance from the wall

Then 2x feet of fence is used for these 2 sides. The side opposite the existing wall would use the remainder of the 200 feet of fence, that is, $200-2x$ feet of fence. Therefore the width (w) of the garden is x feet and the length (l) is $200-2x$ feet.

The area is calculated using the formula a=lw, a=x(200-2x)$= 200x - 2x^2$, and needs to be greater than or equal to 4800 sq. ft., yielding the inequality $4800 \leq 200x - 2x^2$. Subtract 4800 from each side and the inequality becomes $2x^2 - 200x + 4800 \leq 0$ and can be solved for x.

$$200x - 2x^2 \geq 4800$$
$$-2x^2 + 200x - 4800 \geq 0$$
$$2\left(-x^2 + 100x - 2400\right) \geq 0$$
$$-x^2 + 100x - 2400 \geq 0$$
$$(-x + 60)(x - 40) \geq 0$$
$$-x + 60 \geq 0$$
$$-x \geq -60$$
$$x \leq 60$$
$$x - 40 \geq 0$$
$$x \geq 40$$

The area will be at least 4800 square feet if the width of the garden is from 40 up to 60 feet. (The length of the rectangle would vary from 120 feet to 80 feet depending on the width of the garden.)

<u>Example:</u> The height of a projectile fired upward at a velocity of v meters per second from an original height of h meters is $y = h + vx - 4.9x^2$. If a rocket is fired from an original height of 250 meters with an original velocity of 4800 meters per second, find the approximate time the rocket would drop to sea level (a height of 0).

Substituting the height and velocity into the equation yields: $y = 250 + 4800x - 4.9x^2$. If the height at sea level is zero, then $y = 0$ so $0 = 250 + 4800x - 4.9x^2$. Solving for x could be done by using the quadratic formula.

$$x = \frac{-4800 \pm \sqrt{4800^2 - 4(-4.9)(250)}}{2(-4.9)}$$

$$x \approx 979.53 \text{ or } x \approx -0.05 \text{ seconds}$$

Since the time has to be positive, it will be approximately 980 seconds until the rocket reaches sea level.

Skill 7.7   Identify the graph of quadratic functions

The general technique for graphing quadratics is the same as for graphing linear equations. Graphing quadratic equations, however, results in a parabola instead of a straight line.

(see example on the next page)

<u>Example:</u> Graph $y = 3x^2 + x - 2$

x	$y = 3x^2 + x - 2$
-2	8
-1	0
0	-2
1	2
2	12

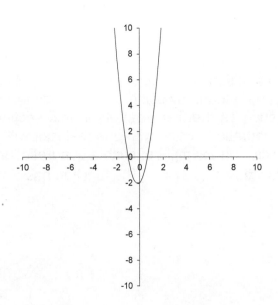

A quadratic function necessarily includes the quadratic term (for instance, x^2) and, possibly, a linear term or a constant term (or both). The general form of a quadratic function is $y = ax^2 + bx + c$

Once a function is identified as quadratic, it is helpful to recognize several features that can indicate the general form of the graph.

The x-coordinate of the vertex (or turning point) of the parabola is given by

$$x = -\frac{b}{2a}.$$

In the equation of the graph shown above, a =3, b=1. The x-coordinate of the vertex is therefore x=-1/6.

If the quadratic term is positive, then the parabola is concave up; if the quadratic term is negative, then the parabola is concave down. The function $-x^2 - 2x - 3$ is one such example and is shown below.

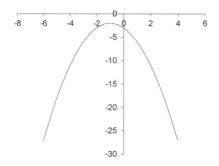

In addition, it is helpful to find the number of roots. The roots of a quadratic equation can be found by using the quadratic formula. A quadratic function with two real roots (such as the first example in this section) will have two crossings of the *x*-axis. A quadratic function with one real root will graph as a parabola that is tangent to the *x*-axis. An example of such a quadratic function is shown in the example below for the function $x^2 + 2x + 1$. The function has a single real root at *x* = –1.

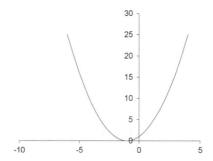

A quadratic function with no real roots will not cross the axis at any point. An example is the function $x^2 + 2x + 2$, which is plotted below.

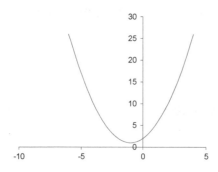

Skill 7.8   Solve equations involving radicals, limited to square roots

To solve a radical equation, isolate the term with a radical on one side of the equation. Raise both sides of the equation to a power equal to the index on the radical. For example, square both sides of an equation containing a square root, or cube both sides of an equation containing a cube root. Do not raise each term to the appropriate power separately; raise the entire side of the equation as a whole. Solve the remaining equation.

Be sure to check the values obtained using this method in the original radical equation. Not every value may satisfy the original equation. If no value satisfies the original equation, then the answer to the equation is $\varnothing$, the empty set or null set.

Example: Solve for x.

$$\sqrt{2x-8} - 7 = 9 \qquad \text{Get radical alone}$$
$$\sqrt{2x-8} = 16$$
$$\left(\sqrt{2x-8}\right)^2 = 16^2 \qquad \text{Square both sides}$$
$$2x - 8 = 256 \qquad \text{Solve for x}$$
$$2x = 264$$
$$x = 132$$

Check:

$$\sqrt{2(132)-8} - 7 = 9$$
$$\sqrt{264-8} - 7 = 9$$
$$\sqrt{256} - 7 = 9$$
$$16 - 7 = 9 \qquad \text{This answer checks.}$$

Example: Solve for x.

$$\sqrt{5x-1} - 1 = x \qquad \text{Add 1.}$$
$$\left(\sqrt{5x-1}\right)^2 = (x+1)^2 \qquad \text{Square both sides.}$$
$$5x - 1 = x^2 + 2x + 1 \qquad \text{Solve this equation.}$$
$$0 = x^2 - 3x + 2$$
$$0 = (x-2)(x-1)$$
$$x = 2 \qquad x = 1$$

Check both answers:

$$\sqrt{5(2)-1} - 1 = 2 \qquad\qquad \sqrt{5(1)-1} - 1 = 1$$
$$3 - 1 = 2 \qquad\qquad\qquad\qquad 2 - 1 = 1$$

Both answers check.

Skill 7.9   Apply the laws of exponents

The **exponent form** is a shortcut method to write repeated multiplication. The **base** is the factor. The **exponent** tells how many times that number is multiplied by itself.

Example: 3^4 is $3 \times 3 \times 3 \times 3 = 81$ where 3 is the base and 4 is the exponent.

x^2 *is read* "x squared"
y^3 *is read* "y cubed"

$a^1 = a$ for all values of a; thus $17^1 = 17$
$b^0 = 1$ for all values of b; thus $24^0 = 1$

When 10 is raised to any power, the exponent tells the number of zeroes in the product.

Example: $10^7 = 10,000,000$

Add the exponents when multiplying like bases. $a^x a^y = a^{x+y}$

Example: $(3^4)(3^5) = 3^9$

Multiply the exponents when raising a power to a power. $(a^x)^y = a^{xy}$

Example: $(2^3)^2 = 2^6$

Subtract the exponents when dividing like bases. $a^x \div a^y = a^{x-y}$

Example: $2^5 \div 2^3 = 2^2$

The product 2 of bases, when they are each raised to the same power, can be multiplied together and become the new base underneath the one exponent. $a^x b^x = (ab)^x$

Example: $(4^2)(5^2) = 20^2$

To make a negative exponent positive, change the base to its reciprocal. $a^{-x} = \dfrac{1}{a^x}$

Example: $2^{-2} = \dfrac{1}{2^2}$

Samples of simplifying expressions with exponents:

$$(-2)^3 = -8 \qquad\qquad (-2)^3 = -1 * (2)^3 = -8$$

$$(-2)^4 = 16 \qquad\qquad (-2)^4 = 1 * (2)^4 = 16 \qquad \text{Note change of sign}$$

$$(2 \div 3)^3 = 2^3 \div 3^3 = 8 \div 27$$

$$(1 \div 3)^{-2} = 3^2 = 9$$

$$4^{-1} = \frac{1}{4}$$

Example: Simplify $\dfrac{3^5\left(3^{-2} + 3^{-3}\right)}{9}$

$$\frac{3^5\left(3^{-2} + 3^{-3}\right)}{9} = \frac{3^5\left(3^{-2} + 3^{-3}\right)}{3^2} = 3^3\left(3^{-2} + 3^{-3}\right)$$

$$= 3^3 3^{-2} + 3^3 3^{-3} = 3^{3-2} + 3^{3-3} = 3 + 1 = 4$$

Example: Simplify $\dfrac{3^2 \cdot 5^{-2} \cdot 2^5}{6^2 \cdot 5}$

$$\frac{3^2 \cdot 5^{-2} \cdot 2^5}{6^2 \cdot 5} = \frac{3^2 \cdot 5^{-2} \cdot 2^5}{3^2 \cdot 2^2 \cdot 5} = 5^{-2-1} \cdot 2^{5-2} = \frac{2^3}{5^3} = \frac{8}{125}$$

COMPETENCY 8   **KNOWLEDGE OF DATA ANALYSIS, STATISTICS, AND PROBABILITY**

Skill 8.1   **Determine which measure of center (i.e. central tendency) is the most appropriate in a given situation**

See Skill 8.2

Skill 8.2   **Find and interpret the range and distribution of data**

Mean, median, and mode are three measures of central tendency. The **mean** is the average of the data items. The **median** is found by putting the data items in order from smallest to largest and selecting the item in the middle (or the average of the two items in the middle). The **mode** is the most frequently occurring item. **Range** is a measure of variability. It is found by subtracting the smallest value from the largest value. **Standard Deviation** expresses how spread out the data is.

Example: Find the mean, median, mode, standard deviation, and range of the test scores listed below:

85	77	65
92	90	54
88	85	70
75	80	69
85	88	60
72	74	95

Mean is the average of all the numbers.

x = sum of all scores ÷ number of scores
  = 1404 ÷ 18
  = 78

Median is the middle number when numbers are arranged in order from smallest to largest. If the set contains an even number of numbers, the two middle numbers are averaged.

54, 60, 65, 69, 70, 72, 74, 75, 77, 80, 85, 85, 85, 88, 88, 90, 92, 95

The numbers 77 and 80 are both in the middle since the total number of scores is even. Therefore, the median is the average of the 2 numbers, or 78.5.

Mode is the most frequently occurring number. The only number that occurs three times in the list of scores is 85. Therefore the mode = 85

Standard Deviation is calculated with the formula $\sqrt{\frac{\Sigma(x-\mu)^2}{n}}$ where n is the number of pieces of data, and $(x - \mu)$ represents the difference between each piece of data and the mean.

$$\sqrt{\frac{(54 - 78.5)^2 + (60 - 78.5)^2 + (69 - 78.5)^2 + (70 - 78.5)^2 + \ldots + (95 - 78.5)^2}{18}}$$

$$\sqrt{\frac{2260.5}{18}} \approx 11.2$$

Range is the largest number minus the smallest number.

= 95 - 54
= 41

Different situations require different information. For instance, if we examine the circumstances under which an ice cream storeowner may use statistics collected in the store, we find different uses for different information.

Over a 7-day period, the storeowner collected data on the ice cream flavors sold. He found the mean number of scoops sold was 174 per day. The most frequently sold flavor (mode) was vanilla. This information was useful in determining how much ice cream to order and the appropriate amount of each flavor.

In the case of the ice cream store, the median and range had little business value for the owner.

Alternatively, consider a set of test scores from a math class: 0, 16, 19, 65, 65, 65, 68, 69, 70, 72, 73, 73, 75, 78, 80, 85, 88, and 92. The mean is 64.06 and the median is 71. Since there are only three scores less than the mean out of the eighteen scores, the median (71) would provide a more valuable assessment of the class' overall performance on the test. A standard deviation of 24.8 indicates that the data is fairly spread out over its range of 92.

Retail storeowners may be most concerned with the most commonly sold dress size (mode), so they may order more of that size than the others.

When analyzing costs of comparable items, measures of central tendency may prove helpful in different ways or under different circumstances. If $250,000; $255,000; $275,000; and $500,000 represent the prices paid for the most recently sold houses in a neighborhood, the median value of $265,000 more fairly represents the neighborhood's worth than the mean price of $320,000 due to the most expensive house being an outlier, or a piece of data somewhat removed from the rest.

Regardless of which measure of central tendency is presented, the values are a unique way to represent a collection of data.

Skill 8.3   Interpret information and patterns from various graphical representations using univariate (e.g., a line plot) and bivariate data (e.g., scatter plot)

Good graphical representation of data communicates many characteristics and trends associated with a set of values. With careful inspection of the type of graph, its range, and its scale, reasonable conclusions can be drawn regarding the data. Such characteristics and trends can be quite valuable insights into the analysis of the data.

Take, for instance, the data presented in the following line plot:

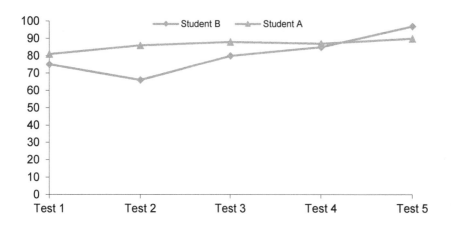

It would be fair to say that Student B has improved over time, while Student A's performance has remained more steady, or unchanged. If Student B's habits continued, one could expect a score for Test 6 to reach even closer to 100.

The previous example describes how one set of measurements, the test scores, can be presented for each student. Additional students would result in added lines to the graph. This would be an example of univariate data because it measures one characteristic, or variable.

Another possible display form for univariate data is a **histogram.** This type of graph is used to summarize the information in a large data set. It shows the counts of data in different ranges. The count in each range or **bin** is known as the **frequency.** The histogram shows graphically the center of the data set, the spread of the data and whether there are any outliers. It also shows whether the data has a single mode or more than one.

<u>Example:</u> The histogram below shows the summary of some test results where people scored points ranging from 0 to 45. The total range of points has been divided into bins 0-5, 6-10, 11-15 and so on. The frequency for the first bin (labeled 5) is the number of people who scored points ranging from 0 to 5; the frequency for the second bin (labeled 10) is the number of people who scored points ranging from 6 to 10 and so on.

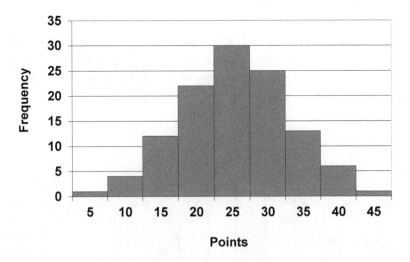

A histogram is a **discrete frequency distribution**. It can be used to represent discrete as well as continuous data (data that can take on a continuous range of values, e.g. height) sorted in bins. A large data set of continuous data may also be represented using a **continuous frequency distribution**, which is essentially a histogram with very narrow bars. Below, a trend line has been added to the example histogram above. Notice that this approximates the most common continuous distribution, a **normal or bell curve**.

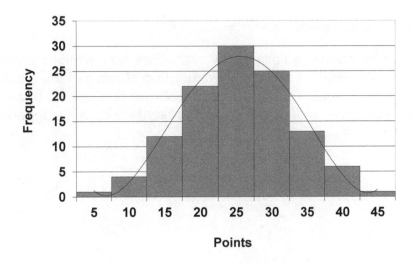

A normal distribution is symmetric with the mean equal to the median. The tails of the curve in both directions fall off rapidly. The spread of data is measured by the standard deviation.

Following are examples of ways in which data represented by a normal curve is interpreted and used. **Percentiles** divide data into 100 equal parts. A person whose score falls in the 65th percentile has outperformed 65 percent of all those who took the test. This does not mean that the score was 65 percent out of 100 nor does it mean that 65 percent of the questions answered were correct. It means that the grade was higher than 65 percent of all those who took the test.

Stanine "standard nine" scores combine the understandability of percentages with the properties of the normal curve of probability. Stanines divide the bell curve into nine sections, the largest of which stretches from the 40th to the 60th percentile and is the "Fifth Stanine" (the average of taking into account error possibilities).

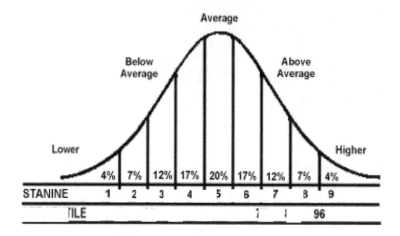

Even though the normal distribution is commonly observed, there are many other kinds of frequency distributions.

http://mathworld.wolfram.com/ContinuousDistribution.html

Other graphical data representations can display two variables, sometimes showing a link between the two measurements. A set of data consisting of two variables can be referred to as bivariate data. A scatter plot like the one shown on the next page can model how a dependent variable, along the y-axis, presents with an independent variable, measured along the x-axis.

This scatter plot could be a display of how distance, on the y-axis, changes over time, across the x-axis.

The line of best fit shows where the data is most likely to occur.

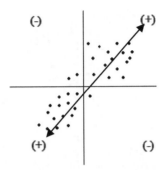

Correlation is a measure of association between two variables. It varies from –1 to 1, with 0 being a random relationship, 1 being a perfect positive linear relationship, and –1 being a perfect negative linear relationship.

The **correlation coefficient** (r) is used to describe the strength of the association between the variables and the direction of the association. A positive r value shows the line of best fit rises, or increases to the right, while a negative r value would indicate falling, or decreasing to the right.

Regression is a form of statistical analysis used to predict a dependent variable (y) from values of an independent variable (x). A regression equation is derived from a known set of data.

If the points in the above scatter plot represented a set of data taken experimentally, the line of best fit would predict the most likely relationship. Comparing distance over time, the slope of the line of best fit would indicate the average velocity in the experiment.

The simplest regression analysis models the relationship between two variables using the equation y = a + bx, where y is the dependent variable and x is the independent variable. This equation denotes a linear relationship between x and y and is appropriately used when a graph of corresponding x and y points roughly forms a straight line.

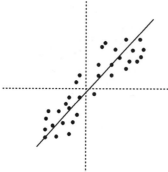

The line can then be used to make predictions.

If all of the data points fell on the line, there would be a perfect correlation ($r = 1.0$) between the x and y data points. These cases represent the best scenarios for prediction. An r value represents how y varies with x. When r is positive, y increases as x increases. When r is negative, y decreases as x increases.

Skill 8.4   Identify appropriate graphical representations for a given data set

Often data is made more readable and user friendly by consolidating the information in the form of a graph.

	Test 1	Test 2	Test 3	Test 4	Test 5
Evans, Tim	75	66	80	85	97
Miller, Julie	94	93	88	97	98
Thomas, Randy	81	86	88	87	90

Bar graphs are used to compare various quantities.

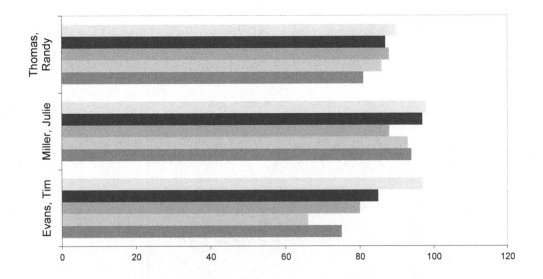

Line graphs are used to show trends, often over a period of time.

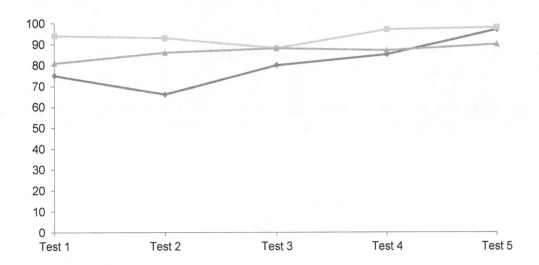

A **pictograph** shows comparison of quantities using symbols. Each symbol represents a number of items.

Example: A class had the following grades: 40 As, 90 Bs, 80 Cs, 10 Ds, 30 Fs. Graph these on a bar graph and a pictograph.

Pictograph

Grade	Number of Students
A	☺☺☺☺
B	☺☺☺☺☺☺☺☺☺
C	☺☺☺☺☺☺☺☺
D	☺
F	☺☺☺

☺ = 10 Students

Circle graphs show the relationship of various parts to each other and the whole. Percents are used to create circle graphs.

Example: Julie spends 8 hours each day in school, 2 hours doing homework, 1 hour eating dinner, 2 hours watching television, 10 hours sleeping and the rest of her time doing other activities.

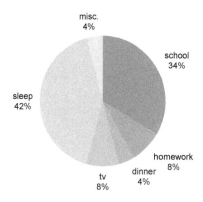

Skill 8.5   Identify an appropriate sample to draw inferences about a population

In probability, the **sample space** is a list of all possible outcomes of an experiment. For example, the sample space of tossing two coins is the set {HH, HT, TT, TH} where heads is H and tails is T and the sample space of rolling a six-sided die is the set {1, 2, 3, 4, 5, 6}.

When analyzing experiments with a large number of possible outcomes, it is important to find the size of the sample space. The size of the sample space can be determined by using the fundamental counting principle and the rules of combinations and permutations.

The **fundamental counting principle** states that if there are m possible outcomes for one task and n possible outcomes of another, there are (m x n) possible outcomes of the two tasks together.

A **permutation** is the number of possible arrangements of items, without repetition, where order of selection is important.

A **combination** is the number of possible arrangements, without repetition, where order of selection is not important.

<u>Example:</u> If any two numbers are selected from the set {1, 2, 3, 4}, list the possible permutations and combinations.

Combinations	Permutations
12, 13, 14, 23, 24, 34	12, 21, 13, 31, 14, 41,
	23, 32, 24, 42, 34, 43,
six ways	twelve ways

Note that the list of permutations includes 12 and 21 as separate possibilities since the order of selection is important. In the case of combinations, however, the order of selection is not important and therefore 12 is the same combination as 21. Hence, 21 is not listed separately as a possibility.

The number of permutations and combinations may also be found by using the formulas given below.

The number of possible permutations in selecting r objects from a set of n is given by

$$_nP_r = \frac{n!}{(n-r)!}$$ The notation $_nP_r$ is read "the number of permutations of n objects taken r at a time."

In our example, 2 objects are being selected from a set of 4.

$$_4P_2 = \frac{4!}{(4-2)!}$$ 　　　Substitute known values.

$$= \frac{4!}{2!} = \frac{4 \cdot 3 \cdot 2 \cdot 1}{2 \cdot 1}$$

$$_4P_2 = 12$$

The number of possible combinations in selecting r objects from a set of n is given by

$$_nC_r = \frac{n!}{(n-r)!r!}$$ 　　The number of combinations when r objects are selected from n objects.

In our example,

$$_4C_2 = \frac{4!}{(4-2)!2!}$$ 　　Substitute known values.

$$= \frac{4!}{2!2!} = \frac{4 \cdot 3 \cdot 2 \cdot 1}{2 \cdot 1 \cdot 2 \cdot 1}$$

$$_4C_2 = 6$$

Example: Find the size of the sample space of rolling two six-sided dice and flipping two coins.

List the possible outcomes of each event:
each dice: {1, 2, 3, 4, 5, 6}
each coin: {Heads, Tails}

Apply the fundamental counting principle: size of sample space = 6 x 6 x 2 x 2 = 144

Example: Find the size of the sample space of selecting three playing cards at random from a standard fifty-two card deck.

Use the rule of combination: $_{52}C_3 = \dfrac{52!}{(52-3)!3!} = 22100$

Proper understanding of the concepts regarding sample space that have been explained thus far is essential to correctly calculating theoretical probability. Experimental probability, however, requires a different understanding of sample space. Since Experimental and Theoretical probabilities will be discussed in the next skill section, an additional note on sample space will be included in that section.

Skill 8.6 Make predictions based on experimental or theoretical probabilities

Probability represents one of the most useful applications in mathematics. When numbers and outcomes can be tracked analyzed and used to predict future outcomes, numerous business and economic decisions can be made with much more confidence. While probability never guarantees an outcome, it offers a high level of reasonable expectation of what may occur.

Decisions and predictions can be made from either experimental or theoretical probability, but it is important to understand the difference between the two.

Consider, then, an experiment conducted by a group of students, where a coin is repeatedly flipped. After each trial, the students recorded which side of the coin landed up: heads or tails. If the experiment was performed 40 times, and heads occurred 27 times, and tails the other 13, the experimental probability of flipping heads would be 27 out of 40.

Theoretically, however, the probability of tossing heads is 1 out of 2, or 50%, since a head is one outcome out of 2 possibilities. With 40 flips, the expectation would be for heads to occur 20 times. This scenario explains that theoretical probability is never guaranteed, but rather a strong indicator of what may happen in a given situation. Experimental probability is calculated from the actual results of a series of trials.

Increasing the amount of times an experiment is repeated, creates a larger sample space. As an experiment's sample size increases, the experimental probability results should grow closer to the theoretical probability calculations, but a perfect match is still not guaranteed.

Additionally, for certain types of experiments, it is essential to ensure the sample space fairly represents the population. For instance, if an experiment is to measure the probability that a bean plant will produce more than 5 beans, the sample space should include an equitable distribution of plants, or plants that experience the same growing conditions.

While experimental probability is calculated from the actual results of repeated trials, theoretical probability takes into consideration the details of the event. These details can range from simple to quite complex.

The most basic construction of a theoretical probability calculation is based on a fraction.

$$\text{Probability} = \frac{\text{number of possible successes}}{\text{total number of possible outcomes}}.$$

Example: Find the theoretical probability of rolling a multiple of 3 on a regular, six sided die.

Rolling a six-sided die has a total of 6 possible outcomes. There are 2 possible successes for this event: rolling a 3 or a 6. Therefore, the probability of rolling a multiple of 3 is 2 out of 6, or 1/3.

Example: Find the theoretical probability of getting all hearts in a 5-card hand from a standard deck.

The sample space for this situation suggests a combination. (See Skill 8.5) The total number of possible 5 card hands is $_{52}C_5$. The number of ways an all-heart hand can be made is $_{13}C_5$. The resulting calculation, $_{13}C_5/_{52}C_5$ yields a probability of .0005 or .05%. When a probability is this low, the chance that such a hand could ever be dealt is virtually zero, and should not be expected.

When probability analysis extends to a series of events, it is essential to recognize the difference between dependent and independent events. Dependent events occur when the probability of the second event depends on the outcome of the first event. Independent events are unrelated and the probability of the second event is not dependent on the first.

For example, consider the two events. (A) It is sunny on Saturday and (B) a person will go to the beach. If the person intends to go to the beach on Saturday, rain or shine, then A and B may be independent. If however, the person plans to go to the beach only if it is sunny, then A and B may be dependent. In this situation, the probability of event B will change depending on the outcome of event A.

Suppose a pair of dice, one red and one green, is rolled. If a three is rolled on the red die and a four on the green die, the events do not depend on each other. The total probability of the two independent events can be found by multiplying the separate probabilities.

$$
\begin{aligned}
P(A \text{ and } B) \quad &= P(A) \times P(B) \\
&= 1/6 \times 1/6 \\
&= 1/36
\end{aligned}
$$

Example: A jar contains 12 red marbles and 8 blue marbles. If a marble is randomly selected and replaced, then a second marble is randomly selected, find the probability of selecting two red marbles.

The selections are independent events, because the probability of picking a red marble the second time remains the same.

P(Red and Red) with replacement = P(Red) × P(Red)
= 12/20 × 12/20
= 9/25

Example: A jar contains 12 red marbles and 8 blue marbles. If a marble is randomly selected and not replaced, then a second marble is randomly selected, find the probability of selecting two red marbles.

If you pick a red marble and pick again without replacing the first red marble, the second pick becomes dependent upon the first pick.

P(Red and Red) without replacement = P_1(Red) × P_2(Red)
= 12/20 × 11/19
= 33/95

Finally, the theoretical probability of some events cannot be determined. For instance, one cannot assume the probability of winning a tennis match is ½ because, in general, winning and losing are not equally likely. In such cases, past results of similar events can be used to help predict future outcomes. The **relative frequency** of an event is the number of times an event has occurred divided by the   number of attempts.

$$\text{relative frequency} = \frac{\text{number of successful trials}}{\text{total number of trials}}$$

For example, if a weighted coin flipped 50 times lands on heads 40 times and tails 10 times, the relative frequency of heads is 40/50 = 4/5. Thus, one can predict that if the coin is flipped 100 times, it will land on heads 80 times.

Example: Two tennis players, John and David, have played each other 20 times. John has won 15 of the previous matches and David has won 5.
    (a) Estimate the probability that David will win the next match.
    (b) Estimate the probability that John will win the next 3 matches.

(a) David has won 5 out of 20 matches. Thus, the relative frequency of David winning is 5/20 or ¼. We can estimate that the probability of David winning the next match is ¼.

(b) John has won 15 out of 20 matches. The relative frequency of John winning is 15/20 or ¾. We can estimate that the probability of John winning a future match is ¾. Thus, the probability that John will win the next three matches is:

$$\frac{3}{4} \times \frac{3}{4} \times \frac{3}{4} = \frac{27}{64}$$

COMPETENCY 9   KNOWLEDGE OF TWO-DIMENSIONAL GEOMETRY

Skill 9.1 **Identify precise definitions of symbols for lines, segments, rays, and distances based on point, line, and plane as undefined terms**

A **point** is a dimensionless location and has no length, width or height.

A **line** connects a series of points and continues "straight" infinitely in two directions. Lines extend in one dimension. A line is defined by any two points that fall on the line, therefore a line may have multiple names.

A **line segment** is a portion of a line. A line segment is the shortest distance between two endpoints and is named using those endpoints. Line segments therefore have exactly two names (i.e., $\overline{AB}$ or $\overline{BA}$). Because line segments have two endpoints, they have a defined length or distance.

A **ray** is a portion of a line that has only one endpoint and continues infinitely in one direction. Rays are named using the endpoint as the first point and any other point on the ray as the second.

Example: Using the diagram below, name the line, line segments, and rays.

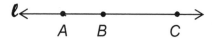

Line: $\overleftrightarrow{AB}, \overleftrightarrow{BA}, \overleftrightarrow{BC}, \overleftrightarrow{CB}, \overleftrightarrow{AC}$ and $\overleftrightarrow{CA}$ all name the line above.

The line above can also be referred to as "line ℓ" given the label to the left.
Line Segments: $\overline{AB}$ or $\overline{BA}$, $\overline{BC}$ or $\overline{CB}$ and $\overline{AC}$ or $\overline{CA}$ name the three line segments.

Ray: $\overrightarrow{AB}$ or $\overrightarrow{AC}$, $\overrightarrow{CB}$ or $\overrightarrow{CA}$, $\overrightarrow{BC}$ and $\overrightarrow{BA}$ name the four rays.

Note that the symbol for a line includes two arrows (indicating infinite extent in both directions), the symbol for a ray includes only one arrow (indicating that it has one endpoint) and the symbol for a line segment has no arrows (indicating two endpoints).

Furthermore, if the symbol above a pair of letters is absent, the letter pair represents the distance between the two endpoints, or the length of the segment.

Example: Use the diagram below, calculate AB given AC is 6 cm and BC is twice as long as AB.

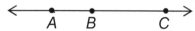

AB + BC = AC
Let x = AB
x + 2x = 6 cm
3x = 6 cm
x = 2 cm, so the length of $\overline{AB}$ is 2 cm.

A **plane** is a flat surface defined by three points. Planes extend indefinitely in two dimensions. A common example of a plane is x-y plane used in the Cartesian coordinate system.

In geometry, the point, line, and plane are key concepts and can be discussed in relation to each other.

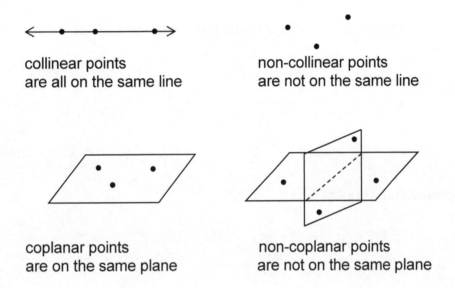

collinear points
are all on the same line

non-collinear points
are not on the same line

coplanar points
are on the same plane

non-coplanar points
are not on the same plane

Any three points on a plane can be used to name the plane. So the plane above can be called Plane ABC or Plane BCA, etc.

The naming of angles can be done with the letters from the angle's rays, or with a labeled number.

Example:

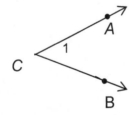

$\overrightarrow{CA}$ (read ray CA) and $\overrightarrow{CB}$ are the sides of the angle.

The angle can be called $\angle ACB$, $\angle BCA$, $\angle C$ or $\angle 1$. Note that when naming the angle with 3 letters, the vertex of the angle must always be in the center of the angle's name.

A lowercase m before the angle symbol is used to indicate the angle's measure. For instance, "the measure of angle one is 12 degrees" can be written as m$\angle 1$ = 12°.

Skill 9.2   **Identify and apply properties of the relationships of angles or pairs of angles**

Properties of angles can be based on their measure or location. Single angles are classified according to their size as follows:

> **acute**:   greater than 0° and less than 90°
> **right**:   exactly 90°
> **obtuse**:   greater than 90° and less than 180°
> **straight**:   exactly 180°

Properties of pairs of angles are recognized by the following relationships:

Adjacent angles have a common vertex and one common side but no interior points in common.

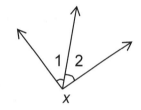

Complementary angles add up to 90°.

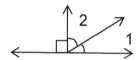

Supplementary angles add up to 180°.

Vertical angles have sides that form two pairs of opposite rays.
Vertical angles have equal measure.

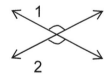

Corresponding angles are in the same corresponding position on two parallel lines cut by a transversal.

Corresponding angles between 2 parallel lines have equal measure.

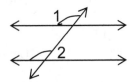

Alternate interior angles are diagonal angles on the inside of two parallel lines cut by a transversal.

Alternate interior angles between 2 parallel lines have equal measure.

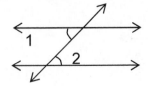

Alternate exterior angles are diagonal angles on the outside of two parallel lines cut by a transversal.

Alternate exterior outside of 2 parallel lines have equal measure.

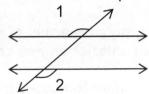

Angle properties can be applied in problem solving.

<u>Examples:</u>

1. If <3 is complementary to <4, and m<3 = 70°, find the m<4.

   Let m<4 = x
   70° + x = 90°
   x = 20°, so the m<4 is 20°

2. Given the diagram to the right,
   with m<1 = 2x, m<2 = x + y + 60°,
   and m<3 = 3y, find the measure of each angle.

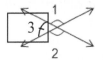

   Since <1 and <2 are vertical angles, they are congruent and their measures are equal: 2x = x + y + 60°, or x = y + 60°

Since <1 and <3 are supplementary, their measures add to 180°.
2x + 3y = 180°.

Using substitution:
$$2(y + 60°) + 3y = 180°$$
$$2y + 120° + 3y = 180°$$
$$5y + 120° = 180°$$
$$5y = 60°$$
$$y = 12° \qquad x = 12° + 60° = 72°$$

Substitute x and y values to find each angle:

m<1 = 2(72°) = 144°, m<2 = 12° + 72° + 60° = 144, m<3 = 3(12°) = 36°

3. If line *l* is parallel to line *m* in the diagram below, and m<5 = 20°, find m<8

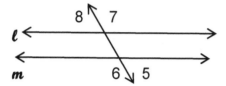

<8 and <5 are alternate exterior angles. When formed by parallel lines, alternate exterior angles are congruent, so m<8 = 20°.

Skill 9.3   Identify and apply properties of polygons to determine the measure(s) of interior angles and/or exterior angles

A **polygon** is a simple closed figure composed of line segments. In a **regular polygon,** all sides are the same length and all angles are the same measure.

The sum of the measures of the **interior angles** of a polygon can be determined using the following formula, where *n* represents the number of angles in the polygon.

Sum of angles = 180°(*n* – 2)

Example: Find the measure of each angle of a regular octagon.

Since an octagon has eight sides, the sum of the angles is: 180°(8 – 2) = 1080°
In a regular octagon, all 8 angles are equal, so each angle measures 1080° ÷ 8 or 135°

The sum of the measures of the **exterior angles** of a polygon, taken one angle at each vertex, equals 360°. Additionally, in a regular polygon, all exterior angles are congruent so the measure of each is 360° ÷ n where *n* represents the number of angles in the polygon.
Example: Find the measure of each interior and exterior angle of a regular pentagon.

A pentagon has five sides, each exterior angle measures:

$$360° \div 5 = 72°$$

Each exterior angle is supplementary to its interior angle, the interior angle measures $180° - 72°$ or $108°$.

While the formula for the sum of the interior angles of a polygon can be used no matter how many sides the polygon has, it is helpful to memorize the sum of the interior angles for one of the most popular polygons in geometry: the triangle.

Since a triangle is a 3 sided polygon, the sum of its interior angles can be calculated by $180° (3 - 2) = 180°$. Therefore, the sum of the measures of the interior angles of a triangle is $180°$.

Example: In a triangle, the measure of the second angle is three times the first. The third angle equals the sum of the measures of the first two angles. What are the measures of each angle?

Let x = the first angle, y = the second angle and z = the third angle
  $y = 3x$
  $z = x + 3x$

Since the sum of the measures of all three angles is $180°$:
$x + y + z = 180°$
$x + 3x + (x + 3x) = 180°$
$8x = 180°$
$x = 22.5°$
$y = 3x = 67.5°$
$z = x + 3x = 90°$

Thus, the angles measure $22.5°$, $67.5°$, and $90°$, and the triangle is a right triangle.

Example: Can a triangle have two right angles?

No. A right angle measures $90°$, therefore the sum of two right angles would be $180°$ and there could not be a third angle.

Example: Can a triangle have two obtuse angles?

No. Since an obtuse angle measures more than $90°$, the sum of two obtuse angles would be greater than $180°$.

Skill 9.4   **Evaluate proofs and apply the properties of triangles (e.g. isosceles, scalene, equilateral)**

A **triangle** is a polygon with three sides.

Triangles can be classified by the types of angles or the lengths of their sides.

Classifying triangles by angles:

An **acute** triangle has exactly three *acute* angles.
A **right** triangle has one *right* angle (and two acute angles).
An **obtuse** triangle has one *obtuse* angle (and two acute angles).

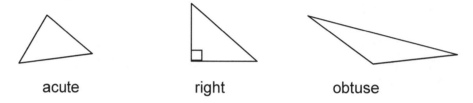

acute   right   obtuse

Classifying triangles by sides:

All *three* sides of an **equilateral** triangle are the same length.
The three angles of an equilateral triangle are equal.
Two sides of an **isosceles** triangle are the same length.
The angles opposite the congruent sides of an isosceles triangle, the base angles, are congruent.
None of the sides of a **scalene** triangle is the same length.

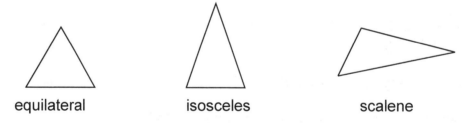

equilateral   isosceles   scalene

Example: If ΔPQR is an equilateral triangle, PQ = 7, and R is the midpoint of $\overline{QM}$, i) find m<PRM and ii) find RM

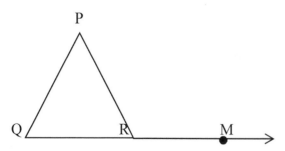

Since the triangle is equilateral, each angle is congruent and measures 180° ÷3 = 60°. Then, since m<PRQ = 60°, and it is supplementary to <PRM, m<PRM = 180° – 60° = 120°

ii) Since the triangle is equilateral, all sides have a length of 7. If R is the midpoint of $\overline{QM}$, then QR = RM = 7.

Example: Given line p is parallel to line m, and m<2 = 90°, prove ΔDRY is a right triangle.

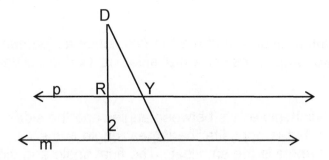

Proof:

1. Line p is parallel to line m<2 = 90°	1. Given
2. <2 ≅ <DRY	2. Corresponding angles formed by parallel lines are congruent.
3. m<DRY = 90°	3. Congruent angles have equal measure.
4. ΔDRY is a right triangle	4. A triangle with a right angle is a right triangle.

Skill 9.5   Evaluate proofs and apply the triangle inequality theorems (e.g., opposite the largest angle is the longest side, the sum of two sides is greater than the third side)

The **Triangle Inequality Theorem** states the sum of the length of any two sides is greater than the length of the remaining side.

If a triangle has an unknown side, the Triangle Inequality Theorem can be applied to determine a reasonable range of possible values for the unknown side.

<u>Example:</u> Determine the range of possible values for the unknown side, *p*.

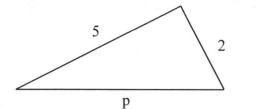

2 + p > 5
2 + 5 > p
p + 5 > 2

The 3 inequalities could be rearranged to show: p > 5–2 or p > 3
p < 7
p > –3

The final inequality yields no information about the triangle, since a side cannot be a negative number. The other two inequalities show that side *p* is a value between 3 and 7, or 3 < p < 7.

Additionally, an angle–side relationship exists between angles and the sides opposite them. The side of the triangle that is opposite the largest angle is the longest side. The side opposite the smallest angle is the smallest. The final angle and side are in between the other two. This rule is used to determine a reasonable measurement of the third unknown angle.

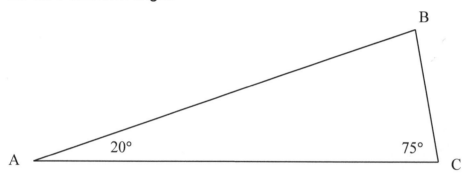

Given the angle measurements in the diagram, and knowing the sum of all angles in a triangle is equal to 180°, $\angle B$ can be calculated.

$\angle A + \angle B + \angle C = 180°$
$20° + \angle B + 75° = 180°$
$\angle B = 180° - 20° - 75°$
$\angle B = 85°$

Given the known angles, $\angle A < \angle C < \angle B$

Then to order the sides according to size, the angle-side relationship can be applied and AC > AB > CB.

<u>Example:</u> Given △ABC is equilateral and m<Y is 20°, prove that $\overline{BY}$ is the longest side of △BOY.

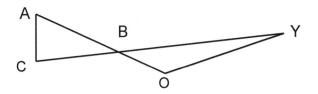

<u>Proof:</u>

1. △ABC is equilateral, m<Y is 20°	1. Given
2. m<ABC = 60°	2. Each angle of an equilateral triangle is 60°
3. m<YBO = 60°	3. Vertical angles have equal measure.
4. m<BOY = 100°	4. 180° – 60° – 20° = 100° biggest angle.
5. $\overline{BY}$ is the longest side of △BOY	5. The longest side of a triangle is across from the biggest angle.

Skill 9.6   Use the SAS, ASA, and SSS postulates to show pairs of triangles congruent, including the case of overlapping triangles

Two triangles can be proven congruent by comparing pairs of appropriate congruent corresponding parts.

SSS Postulate (side-side-side) states if three sides of one triangle are congruent to three sides of another triangle, then the two triangles are congruent.

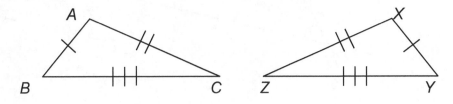

Since $AB \cong XY,\ BC \cong YZ$ and $AC \cong XZ$, then △ABC ≅ △XYZ.

Example: Given isosceles △ABC with D the midpoint of base AC, prove the two triangles formed by BD are congruent.

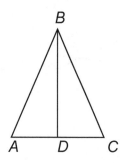

Proof:

1. Isosceles triangle ABC, D midpoint of base AC	1. Given
2. $\overline{AB} \cong \overline{BC}$	2. An isosceles triangle has two congruent sides.
3. $\overline{AD} \cong \overline{DC}$	3. Midpoint divides a line into two equal parts.
4. $\overline{BD} \cong \overline{BD}$	4. Reflexive
5. △ABD ≅ △BCD	5. SSS

SAS Postulate (side-angle-side) states if two sides and the included angle of one triangle are congruent to two sides and the included angle of another triangle, then the two triangles are congruent.

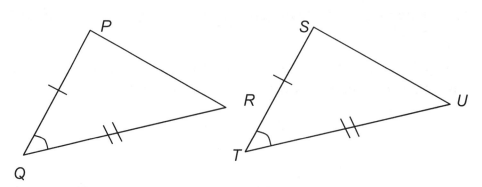

<u>Example</u>: Are the following triangle congruent?

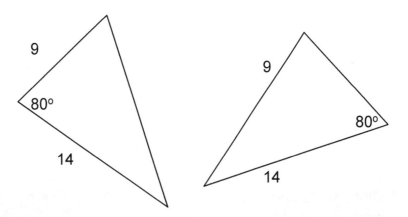

Each of the two triangles has a side that is 14 units and another that is 9 units. The angle included in the sides is 80° in both triangles. Therefore, the triangles are congruent by SAS.

ASA Postulate (angle-side-angle) states if two angles and the included side of one triangle are congruent to two angles and the included side of another triangle, the triangles are congruent.

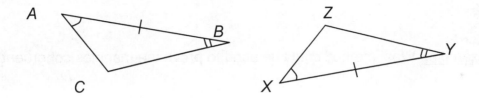

$\angle A \cong \angle X$, $\angle B \cong \angle Y$, $\overline{AB} \cong \overline{XY}$ then $\triangle ABC \cong \triangle XYZ$ by ASA

Example: Given two right triangles with one leg (*AB* and *KL*) of each measuring 6 cm and the adjacent angle 37°, prove the triangles are congruent.

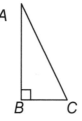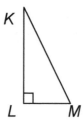

Proof:

1. Right △*ABC* and △*KLM* *AB* = *KL* = 6 cm m∠*A* = m∠*K* = 37°	1. Given
2. $\overline{AB} \cong \overline{KL}$ ∠*A* ≅ ∠*K*	2. Figures with the same measure are congruent
3. ∠*B* ≅ ∠*L*	3. All right angles are congruent
4. △*ABC* ≅ △*KLM*	4. ASA

Example: What method could be used to prove the triangles congruent?

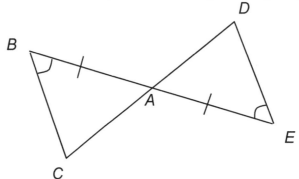

The sides *AB* and *AE* are given as congruent as are ∠*ABC* and ∠*AED*. ∠*BAC* and ∠*DAE* vertical angles and are therefore congruent. By the ASA Postulate △*ABC* and △*AED* are congruent triangles.

<u>Example:</u> ABC is an isosceles triangle with $\overline{AB} \cong \overline{AC}$. An altitude $\overline{BE}$ is drawn from B to $\overline{AC}$. Another altitude $\overline{CD}$ is drawn from C to $\overline{AB}$. Prove that △ CDB and △ BEC are congruent.

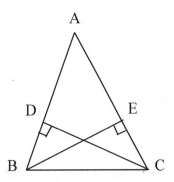

<u>Proof:</u>

1. $\angle ABC \cong \angle ACB$	1. Given that ABC is an isosceles triangle, the base angles are congruent.
2. $\angle BDC = \angle BEC$	2. Given that $\overline{BD}$ and $\overline{CD}$ are altitudes, they form congruent right angles.
3. $\angle EBC = 180° - \angle ACB - \angle BEC$	3. The measures of the three angles of a triangle add up to 180°.
4. $\angle DCB = 180° - \angle DBC - \angle BDC$	4. The measures of the three angles of a triangle add to 180°.
5. $\angle DCB = 180° - \angle ACB - \angle BEC$	5. Substitution
6. $\angle EBC = \angle DCB$	6. Transitive property
7. $\angle EBC \cong \angle DCB$	7. Angles with the same measure are congruent.
8. BC $\cong$ BC	8. Reflexive property
9. $\triangle BDC \cong \triangle CEB$	9. ASA

Skill 9.7   **Apply theorems and postulates that apply to right triangles to solve mathematical and realistic problems. (e.g., Pythagorean Theorem, special right triangles**

The **Pythagorean Theorem** states that, in a right triangle, the square of the length of the hypotenuse is equal to the sum of the squares of the lengths of the legs. Symbolically, it is stated as:

$a^2 + b^2 = c^2$, where a and b are the lengths of the legs, and c is the length of the hypotenuse.

<u>Example:</u> Given the right triangle below, find the hypotenuse.

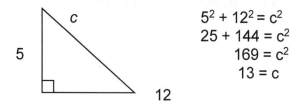

$$5^2 + 12^2 = c^2$$
$$25 + 144 = c^2$$
$$169 = c^2$$
$$13 = c$$

The **converse** of the Pythagorean Theorem states if the square of one side of a triangle is equal to the sum of the squares of the other two sides, then the triangle is a right triangle.

<u>Example:</u> A triangle has sides measuring 12, 16 and 20 cm. Is it a right triangle?

$$c^2 = a^2 + b^2$$
$$20^2 \ \underline{?} \ 12^2 + 16^2$$
$$400 \ \underline{?} \ 144 + 256$$
$$400 \ = 400$$

Yes, the triangle is a right triangle.

This theorem can be expanded to determine if triangles are obtuse or acute.

If the square of the longest side of a triangle is greater than the sum of the squares of the other two sides, then the triangle is an obtuse triangle.

If the square of the longest side of a triangle is less than the sum of the squares of the other two sides, the triangle is an acute triangle.

<u>Example:</u> A triangle has sides measuring 7, 12, and 14 in. Is the triangle right, acute, or obtuse?

$$14^2 \ \underline{?} \ 7^2 + 12^2$$
$$196 \ \underline{?} \ 49 + 144$$
$$196 > 193$$

Therefore, the triangle is obtuse.

Example: An interior quadrangle in an office building has a diagonal pathway going from one corner to another. If the length of the quadrangle is 12m and its width is 9m, what is the length of the pathway?

Draw and label sketch. The diagonal pathway is the hypotenuse of a right triangle with the length and width of the quadrangle as its sides.

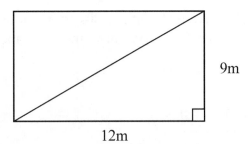

9m

12m

Use the Pythagorean Theorem to find the hypotenuse: $a^2 + b^2 = c^2$

$$9^2 + 12^2 = c^2 \rightarrow c = 15$$

Check:

$$9^2 + 12^2 = 15^2 \rightarrow 81 + 144 = 225$$

Thus, the length of the diagonal pathway is 15m.

Example: A pole is placed in the ground and is 12 ft. in height above ground. A rope tied to the top of the pole is attached to a stake on the ground 5 ft from the base of the pole. If the length of the rope from the top of the pole to the stake is 12.8 ft, is the pole exactly vertical?

Draw and label a diagram:

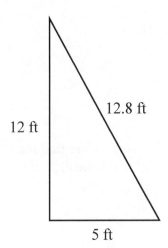

12.8 ft

12 ft

5 ft

If the pole AB is exactly vertical, it will be at right angles to the ground and we should be able to find the length of the rope AC using the Pythagorean Theorem.

Thus, if AB is vertical, $12^2 + 5^2 = 12.8^2$
                  but $169 \neq 163.84$

Therefore, the pole is not exactly vertical.

Special right triangles have set relationships between the hypotenuse and the legs.

The first of these is a **30°-60°-90° right triangle**. In the diagram below the short leg (*sl*) is opposite the 30° angle, the long leg (*ll*) is opposite the 60° angle and *h* is the hypotenuse.

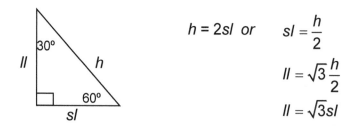

$$h = 2sl \quad or \quad sl = \frac{h}{2}$$

$$ll = \sqrt{3}\,\frac{h}{2}$$

$$ll = \sqrt{3}sl$$

Example: Find the length of the legs of the 30°-60°-90° right triangle.

Since $h = 2sl$, 10 = 2a, so a = 5

and $ll = \sqrt{3}sl$ means $x = \sqrt{3}(5)$

so $x = 5\sqrt{3}$ or 8.66

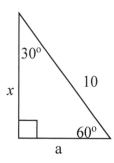

Example: A 20 ft ladder is propped up against a wall. If the distance from the bottom of the ladder to the wall is half the length of the ladder, how high up the wall is the top of the ladder?

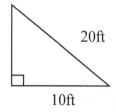

Since the length of the shorter leg of a **30°-60°-90° right triangle** is half the length of the hypotenuse, the ladder forms a 30°-60°-90° right triangle with the wall and ground.

Thus, the longer leg of the right triangle = $\sqrt{3}(10)$ and the top of the ladder is placed 17.3 ft up the wall.

The second special right triangle is a **45°-45°-90° right triangle**. In the diagram below, the legs (*l*) are opposite the 45° angle and *h* is the hypotenuse.

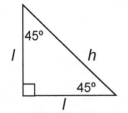

$$l = \frac{h}{\sqrt{2}} \quad \text{or } h = l\sqrt{2}$$

<u>Example</u>: Find the length of the hypotenuse of the 45°-45°-90° right triangle.

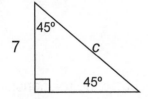

Since $h = l\sqrt{2}$, $c = 7\sqrt{2} \approx 9.899$

<u>Example</u>: A woman is making a scarf in the shape of a right triangle. She wants the two shorter sides to be equal in length and the long side to be 15 inches long. What should the length of each of the shorter sides be?

Since the two shorter sides are equal in length, the scarf is an isosceles right triangle, i.e. a 45°-45°-90° right triangle.

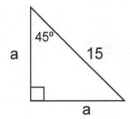

Since $h = a\sqrt{2}$,

$$15 = a\sqrt{2}$$

$$\frac{15}{\sqrt{2}} = a$$

$$a \approx 10.61$$

Skill 9.8   Apply trigonometric ratios to solve right triangle problems

When working with trigonometric functions, it is important to understand the terminology. For right $\triangle ABC$, the adjacent side and opposite side can be identified for $\angle A$ and $\angle B$.

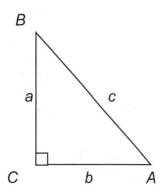

Side b is adjacent to $\angle A$ and side a is opposite $\angle A$. Side a is adjacent to $\angle B$ and side b is opposite $\angle B$.

The longest side, c (opposite the 90° angle), is always called the hypotenuse. The basic trigonometric ratios are listed below:

$\sin \theta$ = opposite/hypotenuse $\csc \theta = 1/\sin \theta$
$\cos \theta$ = adjacent/hypotenuse $\sec \theta = 1/\cos \theta$
$\tan \theta$ = opposite/adjacent $\cot \theta = 1/\tan \theta$

The mnemonic SOHCAHTOA can be used to remember the basic trig relationships: **S**in**O**pp/**H**yp**C**os**A**dj/**H**yp**T**an**O**pp/**A**dj

Example: Use $\triangle ABC$ to find the sin, cos and tan for $\angle A$.

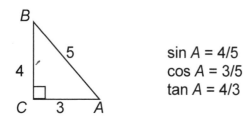

$\sin A = 4/5$
$\cos A = 3/5$
$\tan A = 4/3$

Example: Use a calculator to confirm the approximations for the following:

i) $\sin(87°)$ .9986
ii) $\sin(18°)$ .3090
iii) $\cos(90°)$ 0
iv) $\cos(18°)$ .9511
v) $\sin^{-1}(0.5)$ 30°
vi) $\tan^{-1}(5/12)$ 22.6°

Note: Be sure your calculator is set in degrees.
Traditionally, trig values are rounded to 4 places after the decimal and angles to the nearest whole or tenth of a degree.

Such calculator approximations are used to compute the following examples.

Example: Solve for the missing *side x* of right $\triangle ABC$.

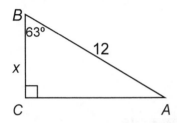

Use cosine to find the adjacent side when the length of the hypotenuse is known.
$\cos 63° = x/12$, $.45399 = x/12$, $x = 5.45$

Example: Find the measure of $\angle A$.

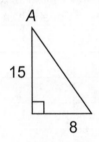

$\tan A = 8/15$
$A = \tan^{-1}(8/15) \approx 28.1°$

Example: Find the length of side *x*.

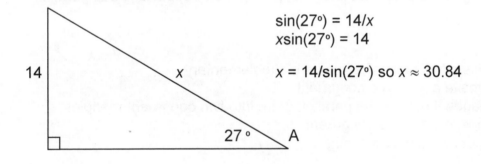

$\sin(27°) = 14/x$
$x\sin(27°) = 14$

$x = 14/\sin(27°)$ so $x \approx 30.84$

Example: Find the length of side x.

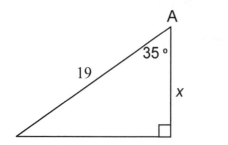

$\cos(35°) = x/19$

$19\cos(35°) = x$

$x \approx 15.6$

Skill 9.9   **Apply the specific properties of quadrilaterals (e.g. parallelograms, rectangles, rhombuses, squares, kites, trapezoids)**

	Parallel Opposite Sides	Bisecting Diagonals	Equal Opposite Sides	Equal Opposite Angles	Equal Diagonals	All Sides Equal	All Angles Equal	Perpendicular Diagonals
Parallelogram	X	X	X	X				
Rectangle	X	X	X	X	X		X	
Rhombus	X	X	X	X		X		X
Square	X	X	X	X	X	X	X	X

**The table above illustrates the properties of each quadrilateral.

A **parallelogram** is a quadrilateral with both pairs of opposite sides parallel.

Theorems:

1. Consecutive pairs of angles are supplementary.
2. Opposite angles are congruent.
3. A diagonal divides the parallelogram into two congruent triangles.
4. Opposite sides are congruent.
5. Diagonals bisect each other.

Example: Given parallelogram $ABCD$ with diagonals AC and BD intersecting at E, prove $\overline{AE} \cong \overline{CE}$.

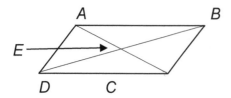

Proof:

1. Parallelogram *ABCD*, with diagonals $\overline{AC}$ and $\overline{BD}$ intersecting at *E*	1. Given
2. $\overline{AB} \parallel \overline{DC}$	2. Opposite sides of a parallelogram are parallel
3. $\angle BDC \cong \angle ABD$ angles are congruent.	3. If parallel lines are cut by a transversal, their alternate interior angles are congruent.
4. $\overline{AB} \cong \overline{DC}$	4. Opposite sides of a parallelogram are congruent.
5. $\angle BAC \cong \angle ACD$	5. If parallel lines are cut by a transversal, their alternate interior angles are congruent.
6. $\triangle ABE \cong \triangle CDE$	6. ASA
7. $\overline{AE} \cong \overline{CE}$	7. Corresponding parts of congruent triangles are congruent.
8. *ABCD* is a parallelogram	8. If both pairs of opposite sides of a quadrilateral are congruent, the quadrilateral is a parallelogram.

A **rectangle** is a parallelogram with a right angle (making all angles right angles).

All rectangles are parallelograms and have all the properties of parallelograms. In addition, all four angles are right angles and the diagonals are congruent.

A **rhombus** is a parallelogram with all sides of equal length.

Rhombuses have all the properties of parallelograms.
In addition, a rhombus is equilateral, the diagonals are perpendicular, and the diagonals bisect the angles.

A **square** is a rectangle with all sides of equal length.

Squares have all the properties of rectangles and all the properties of rhombuses.

A **trapezoid** is a quadrilateral with <u>exactly</u> one pair of opposite sides parallel. The parallel sides are called bases; the non-parallel sides are legs.

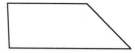

In an **isosceles trapezoid,** the legs are congruent.

An **altitude** is a line segment drawn from a point on either base, perpendicular to the opposite base. The **median** is a line segment that joins the midpoints of each leg.

Theorems:

1. The median of a trapezoid is parallel to the bases and equal to one-half the sum of the lengths of the bases.
2. The base angles of an isosceles trapezoid are congruent.
3. The diagonals of an isosceles trapezoid are congruent.

<u>Example:</u> If TRAP is a trapezoid and m<RAP= 40°, find m<TPA

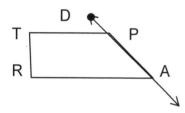

Since TRAP is a trapezoid, $\overleftrightarrow{TP}$ is parallel to $\overleftrightarrow{RA}$. Then <DPT ≅ <RAP because corresponding angles are congruent. With<DPT ≅ <RAP, m<DPT = 40°. <DPT is supplementary to <TPA, so m<TPA = 140°.

Skill 9.10   Apply formulas for distance and midpoint on the coordinate plane

The **distance formula** is used to find the distance (*D*) between two points (x_1, y_1) and (x_2, y_2). The key to applying the distance formula is to understand the problem before beginning.

$$D = \sqrt{(x_2 - x_1)^2 + (y_2 - y_1)^2}$$

<u>Example:</u> Find the perimeter of a figure with vertices at (4, 5), (-4, 6) and ($-5, -8$).

The figure being described is a triangle. Therefore, the distance for all three sides must be found. Identify all three sides before beginning.

Side $1 = (4,5)$ to $(-4,6)$
Side $2 = (-4,6)$ to $(-5,-8)$
Side $3 = (-5,-8)$ to $(4,5)$

$$D_1 = \sqrt{(-4-4)^2 + (6-5)^2} = \sqrt{65}$$

$$D_2 = \sqrt{((^-5-(^-4))^2 + (^-8-6)^2} = \sqrt{197}$$

$$D_3 = \sqrt{((4-(^-5))^2 + (5-(^-8)^2} = \sqrt{250} \text{ or } 5\sqrt{10}$$

$$\text{Perimeter} = \sqrt{65} + \sqrt{197} + 5\sqrt{10}$$

The **midpoint** of a segment is the point on a segment exactly equidistant from the two endpoints.

If a line segment has endpoints of (x_1, y_1) and (x_2, y_2), then the midpoint can be found using:

$$\left(\frac{x_1 + x_2}{2}, \frac{y_1 + y_2}{2} \right)$$

<u>Example:</u> Find the center of a circle with a diameter whose endpoints are (3, 7) and ($-4, -5$).

$$\text{Midpoint} = \left(\frac{3 + (-4)}{2}, \frac{7 + (-5)}{2} \right)$$

$$\text{Midpoint} = \left(\frac{-1}{2}, 1 \right)$$

Example: Find the midpoint given the two points $\left(5, 8\sqrt{6}\right)$ and $\left(9, -4\sqrt{6}\right)$.

$$\text{Midpoint} = \left(\frac{5+9}{2}, \frac{8\sqrt{6} + (-4\sqrt{6})}{2}\right)$$

$$\text{Midpoint} = \left(7, 2\sqrt{6}\right)$$

Skill 9.11 Classify and apply the types of transformations of geometric figures including similar figures

A **transformation** is a change in the position, shape, or size of a geometric figure. **Transformational geometry** is the study of manipulating objects by flipping, twisting, turning, and scaling.

Symmetry exists if a figure is reflected or flipped across a line and appears unchanged. The line where the reflection occurs is known as the **line of symmetry**.

A **translation** is a transformation that "slides" an object a fixed distance in a given direction. The original object and its translation have the same shape and size, and they face in the same direction.

An example of a translation in architecture would be stadium seating. The seats are the same size and the same shape and face in the same direction.

Example: The coordinates $B(4,3), C(4,0), D(0,3)$ make $\triangle BCD$. Find the coordinates of $\triangle B'C'D'$ if $\triangle BCD$ is translated 4 units to the left (minus 4 units on x) and one unit up (plus 1 unit on y):

$\triangle BCD$	$\triangle B'C'D'$
(4,3)	(0,4)
(4,0)	(0,1)
(0,3)	(-4,4)

After adding -4 to each x value and 1 to each y value.

Graphing the original and the result together shows the translation of the triangle. Note that the triangles are still the same size and shape and are, therefore, congruent.

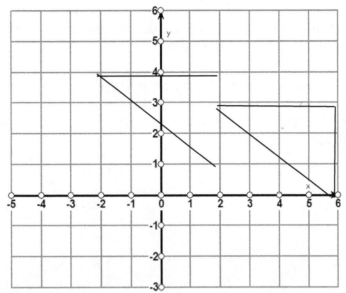

Applying a **scale factor** to a shape is another form of geometric transformation. The scale factor is a multiplier that shrinks or expands a given figure into a new figure. The new figure keeps the same shape as its original, but all corresponding sides are proportionally changed. Therefore, when a scale factor is applied to create a new figure, the result is a pair of similar figures. When used as a ratio to form a proportion, the scale factor may be used to derive the measurements of one shape from the other.

Example: 1) A scale factor of 0.5 is applied to ΔFUN to create ΔABC. Find AC.
2) If the perimeter of ΔFUN = 44, find the perimeter of ΔABC

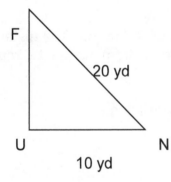

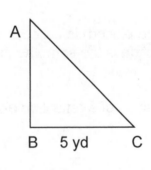

1) The problem can be solved by setting up the proportion below and solving for AC.

$$\frac{AC}{20 \text{ yd}} = \frac{5 \text{ yd}}{10 \text{ yd}}$$

After cross-multiplying, the equation can be written as 10AC = 100; AC equals 10 yards. Alternatively, the scale factor can be applied to the side in question. Since $\overline{FN}$

corresponds to $\overline{AC}$, apply the scale factor to the length of $\overline{FN}$: 20(0.5) = 10. So the length of $\overline{AC}$ is 10 yd.

2) The perimeters of similar figures are also proportional, or related by the scale factor. So the perimeter of $\triangle ABC$ = (.5)44 = 22

A **rotation** is a transformation that turns a figure about a fixed point called the center of rotation. An object and its rotation are the same shape and size, but the figures may be turned in different directions. Rotations can occur in either a clockwise or a counterclockwise direction.

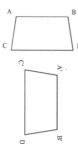

Rotations can be seen in wallpaper and art. A Ferris wheel is an example of rotation.

An object and its **reflection** have the same shape and size, but the figures face in opposite directions.

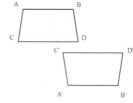

The line (where a mirror may be placed) is called the **line of reflection**. The distance from a point to the line of reflection is the same as the distance from the point's image to the line of reflection.

A **glide reflection** is a combination of a reflection and a translation.

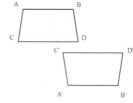

Another type of transformation is **dilation**. Dilation is a transformation that shrinks or enlarges, while preserving the original center.

Example: Using dilation to transform a diagram.

Starting with a triangle whose center of dilation is point P,

we dilate the lengths of the sides by the same factor to create a new triangle.

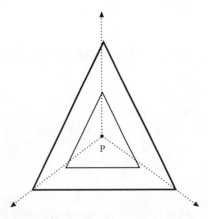

Skill 9.12   Apply properties and theorems about circles

A **circle** is the set of all points equidistant from a given point, P. That point P is the center of the circle and any segment from the center to the edge of the circle is a **radius**. Since all points on the circle are equidistant from the center, all radii of a given circle are congruent.

Any segment drawn across a circle that goes through the center of the circle is a **diameter** of the circle. A circle's diameter is equal to twice the length of its radius. ($d = 2r$)

The distance around a circle is the **circumference**. The ratio of the circumference to the diameter is represented by the Greek letter pi (π).

$$\pi \approx 3.14$$

The **circumference** of a circle is found by the formula $C = 2\pi r$ or $C = \pi d$ where r is the radius of the circle and d is the diameter.

The **area** of a circle is found by the formula $A = \pi r^2$.

Example: Find the circumference and area of a circle whose radius is 7 meters.

7 m

$$C = 2\pi r \qquad\qquad A = \pi r^2$$
$$= 2(3.14)(7\text{ m}) \qquad\qquad = 3.14(7\text{m})^2$$
$$= 43.96\text{ m} \qquad\qquad = 153.86\text{ m}^2$$

<u>Example:</u> Find the surface area of one side of the circular flat washer shown below.

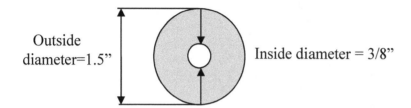

Outside diameter=1.5"

Inside diameter = 3/8"

Area of larger circle (A_1)   Area of smaller circle (A_2)

$$A_1 = \pi r_1^2 \qquad\qquad A_2 = \pi r_2^2$$

$A_1 = \pi(0.75\text{ in.})^2 \qquad\qquad A_2 = \pi(0.1875\text{ in.})^2$

$A_1 = 1.76625\text{ in.}^2 \qquad\qquad A_2 = 0.1103906\text{ in.}^2$

Area of metal washer $= A_1 - A_2$
$$= 1.76625\text{ in.}^2 - 0.1103906\text{ in.}^2$$
$$= 1.6558594\text{ in.}^2$$

Arc Length and Sector Area

An arc of a circle has a measure associated with the degree measure of its central angle. Its length is also a fraction of the circumference of the circle.

Each central angle and its associated arc form a sector of the circle that resembles a pie piece. The area of such a sector is a fraction of the area of the circle.

The fractions used for the area of a sector and the length of its associated arc are both equal to the ratio of the central angle to 360°.

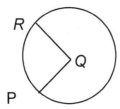

$$\frac{\text{m} < PQR}{360°} = \frac{\text{length of arc RP}}{\text{circumference of circle Q}} = \frac{\text{area of sector PQR}}{\text{area of circle Q}}$$

<u>Example:</u> Circle A has a radius of 4 centimeters. BD is a diameter of the circle. What is the length of arc ED?

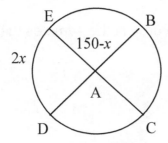

First, find the value of x. Since arc *BE* and arc *DE* form a semicircle,

$$2x + 150 - x = 180°$$
$$x + 150 = 180°$$
$$x = 30°$$

Arc ED = 2(30°) = 60°

The ratio of 60° to 360° is equal to the ratio of arc length *ED* to the circumference of circle A.

$$\frac{60°}{360°} = \frac{arc\ length\ ED}{2\pi 4}$$

$$\frac{1}{6} = \frac{arc\ length\ ED}{8\pi}$$

Cross-multiply and solve for the arc length.

$$arc\ length\ ED = \frac{8\pi}{6}$$

Simplifying, arc length $ED = \dfrac{4\pi}{3}$ cm.

<u>Example:</u> The radius of circle M is 3 centimeters. The length of arc PF is 2π centimeters. What is the area of sector PMF?

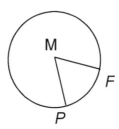

Circumference of circle $M = 2\pi(3) = 6\pi$

Area of circle $M = \pi(3)^2 = 9\pi$

The ratio of the sector area to the circle area is the same as the ratio of the arc length to the circumference.

$$\frac{\text{area of } PMF}{9\pi} = \frac{2\pi}{6\pi}$$

$$\frac{\text{area of } PMF}{9\pi} = \frac{1}{3}$$

Cross multiply and solve: area of $PMF = \dfrac{9\pi}{3}$, area of $PMF = 3\pi$.

COMPETENCY 10   **KNOWLEDGE OF MEASUREMENT AND SPATIAL SENSE**

Skill 10.1   **Convert units of measure within and between given measurement systems including derived units**

The customary units of **length** are inches, feet, yards and miles.

> 12 inches (in) = 1 foot (ft)
> 36 in = 1 yard (yd)
> 3 ft = 1 yd
> 5280 ft = 1 mile (mi)
> 1760 yd = 1 mi

To convert from one unit to another, either set up a proportion, or multiply by the appropriate conversion factor. Examples of each method are shown below.

<u>Example:</u> 4 mi = _____ yd

Using a proportion:

$$\frac{1\,mile}{1760\,yd} = \frac{4\,miles}{x\,yd}$$

$$x = 4 \cdot 1760 = 7040\,yd$$

Multiplying by a conversión factor:

$$4\,mi \cdot \frac{1760\,yd}{1\,mi} = 7040\,yd$$

<u>Example:</u> 21 in = _____ ft

Using a proportion:

$$\frac{12\,in}{1\,ft} = \frac{21\,in}{x\,ft}$$

$$12x = 21$$

$$x = 1.75\,ft$$

Multiplying by a conversion factor:

$$21\,in \cdot \frac{1\,ft}{12\,in} = 1.75\,ft$$

The customary units of **weight** are ounces, pounds and tons.

16 ounces (oz.) = 1 pound (lb)
2000 lb. = 1 ton (T)

Example: 2 T = _____ lb

$$2\,T \cdot \frac{2000\ lb}{1\ T} = 4000\ lb$$

The customary units of **capacity** are fluid ounces, cups, pints, quarts and gallons.

8 fluid ounces (fl oz) = 1 cup (c)
2 c = 1 pint (pt)
4 c = 1 quart (qt)
2 pt = 1 qt
4 qt = 1 gallon (gal)

Example: 3 gal = _____ qt

$$\frac{4\ qt}{1\ gal} = \frac{x\ qt}{3\ gal}$$

$$x = 12\ qt$$

Example: 10 oz = _____ c

$$10\ oz \cdot \frac{1\ c}{8\ oz} = 1.25\ c = 1\frac{1}{4}\ c$$

Square units can be derived with knowledge of basic units of length by squaring the equivalent measurements.

1 square foot (sq ft or ft^2) = 144 sq in
1 sq yd = 9 sq ft
1 sq yd = 1296 sq in

Example: 14 sq yd = _____ sq ft

$$14\ yd^2 \cdot \frac{9\ ft^2}{1\ yd^2} = 126\ ft^2$$

The **metric system** is based on multiples of ten. Conversions are made by simply moving the decimal point to the left or right.

kilo-   1000   thousands
hecto- 100   hundreds
deca-   10   tens
unit   1
deci-   0.1   tenths
centi- 0.01   hundredths
milli- 0.001   thousandths

The basic metric unit for **length** is the meter. One meter is approximately one yard.

The basic metric unit for **weight** or mass is the gram. A paper clip weighs about one gram.

The basic metric unit for **volume** is the liter. One liter is approximately a quart.

These are the most commonly used metric equivalents.

1 cm = 10 mm		
1 m = 1000 mm	1000 mL= 1 L	1000 mg = 1 g
1 m = 100 cm	1 kL = 1000 L	1 kg =1000 g
1000 m = 1 km		

Alternatively, the list of metric prefixes ordered from left to right can aid in conversion.

K H D U D C M

Example: 63 km = _____ m
Since there are 3 steps from Kilo to Unit, move the decimal point 3 places to the right.

63 km = 63,000 m

Example: 14 mL = _____ L
Since there are 3 steps from Milli to Unit, move the decimal point 3 places to the left.

14 mL = 0.014 L

Example: 56.4 cm = _____ mm
56.4 cm = 564 mm

Example: 9.1 m = _____ km
9.1 m = 0.0091 km

When conversion between measurement systems is required, additional conversion factors are needed. Some of the more popular values are:

1 mile = 1.6 km
1 inch = 2.5 cm
1 pound = .45 kg
1 quart = .95 L
1 gallon = 3.8 L

The factor can be set into a proportion for ease of use in either direction.

Example: How many liters are in 2 quarts?

$$\frac{1\ qt}{0.95L} = \frac{2\ qt}{x\ L}$$

$x = 1.9$ L

Example: How many miles are in a 5K (kilometer) run?

$$\frac{1\ mi}{1.6\ km} = \frac{x\ mi}{5\ km}$$

$1.6x = 5$

$x = 3.125$ mi.

Derived units represent combinations of measures. For example, velocity can be measured in meters per second (m/s) or miles per hour (mph). Conversion of these more complicated units is best done by following unit cancellation techniques.

For example, if 25 mph needs to be converted to ft/sec, note the following chain of factors:

$$\frac{25\ miles}{1\ hour} \cdot \frac{5280\ feet}{1\ mile} \cdot \frac{1\ hour}{60\ minutes} \cdot \frac{1\ minute}{60\ seconds} = 36.67\frac{feet}{seconds}$$

Within the above calculation, not only do the numbers multiply and divide to reach the answer, but the units themselves divide each other out along the way, (i.e. miles divided by mile equals 1) leaving the answer with "feet" in the numerator and "seconds" in the denominator, forming the requested unit.

Skill 10.2   Solve realistic and mathematical problems involving perimeter, circumference, area, surface area, and volume

The **perimeter** of any polygon is the sum of the lengths of the sides.

$$P = \text{sum of sides}$$

Since the opposite sides of a rectangle are congruent, the perimeter of a rectangle equals twice the sum of the length and width or

$$P_{rect} = 2l + 2w \text{ or } 2(l + w)$$

Similarly, because all the sides of a square have the same measure, the perimeter of a square equals four times the length of one side or

$$P_{square} = 4s$$

The **area** of a polygon is the number of square units covered by the figure.

$$A_{rect} = l \times w$$
$$A_{square} = s^2$$

Example: Find the perimeter and the area of the rectangle below.

16 cm

9cm

$$
\begin{aligned}
P_{rect} &= 2l + 2w \\
&= 2(16 \text{ cm}) + 2(9 \text{ cm}) \\
&= 32 \text{ cm} + 18 \text{ cm} = 50 \text{ cm}
\end{aligned}
\qquad
\begin{aligned}
A_{rect} &= l \times w \\
&= 16 \text{ cm}(9 \text{ cm}) \\
&= 144 \text{ cm}^2
\end{aligned}
$$

Example: Find the perimeter and area of this square.

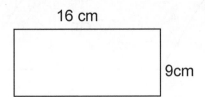

3.6 in

$$
\begin{aligned}
P_{square} &= 4s \\
&= 4(3.6 \text{ in}) \\
&= 14.4 \text{ in}
\end{aligned}
\qquad
\begin{aligned}
A_{square} &= s^2 \\
&= (3.6 \text{ in.})^2 \\
&= 12.96 \text{ in}^2
\end{aligned}
$$

<u>Example:</u> Find the length of landscape edging needed to surround a circular garden with a diameter of 8 ft.

The path of the edging will trace the perimeter of the garden. Perimeter of a circle is the same thing as circumference, which was discussed in Skill 9.12.

$$C = \pi d$$
$$= 3.14(8)$$
$$= 25.12 \text{ ft of edging}$$

The **area** of other polygons can be found using the following formulas, where b = the base and h = the height of an altitude drawn to the base.

$$A_{parallelogram} = bh$$

$$A_{triangle} = (½)bh$$

$$A_{trapezoid} = \frac{1}{2}h(b_1 + b_2)$$

<u>Example:</u> Find the area of a parallelogram whose base is 6.5 cm. The height of the altitude to that base is 3.7 cm.

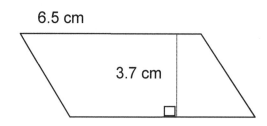

$$A_{parallelogram} = bh$$
$$= (3.7 \text{ cm})(6.5 \text{ cm})$$
$$= 24.05 \text{ cm}^2$$

<u>Example:</u> Find the area of this triangle.

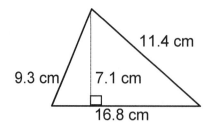

$$A_{triangle} = (½)bh$$
$$= 0.5(16.8 \text{ cm})(7.1 \text{ cm})$$
$$= 59.64 \text{ cm}^2$$

Note that the altitude is drawn to the base measuring 16.8 cm. The lengths of the other two sides are not needed to calculate the area.

Example: Find the area of a right triangle whose sides measure 10 inches, 24 inches and 26 inches.

The hypotenuse of a right triangle must be the longest side. The two perpendicular legs measure 10 inches and 24 inches. These legs are the base and height.

$$A_{triangle} = (½)bh$$
$$= 0.5(10 \text{ in.})(24 \text{ in.})$$
$$= 120 \text{ sq. in.}$$

Example: Find the area of the trapezoid below.

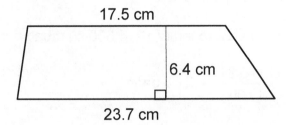

$$A_{trapezoid} = \frac{1}{2}h(b_1 + b_2)$$
$$= \frac{1}{2}(6.4)(17.5 + 23.7)$$
$$= 131.84 \text{ cm}^2$$

Example: A homeowner decided to fertilize her lawn. The shapes and dimensions of the lot, house, pool, and garden are given in the diagram below. The shaded area will not be fertilized. If each bag of fertilizer costs $7.95 and covers 4,500 square feet, find the total number of bags needed and the total cost of the fertilizer.

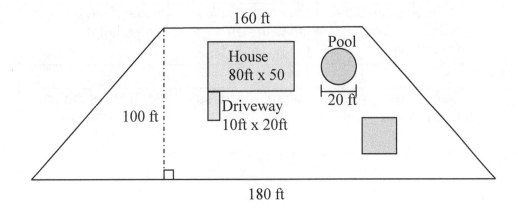

Area of Lot	Area of House	Area of Driveway
$A = \frac{1}{2}\, h(b_1 + b_2)$	$A = LW$	$A = LW$
$A = \frac{1}{2}(100)(180 + 160)$	$A = (80)(50)$	$A = (10)(20)$
$A = 17{,}000$ sq. ft.	$A = 4{,}000$ sq. ft.	$A = 200$ sq. ft.

Area of Pool	Area of Garden
$A = \pi r^2$	$A = s^2$
$A = \pi (10)^2$	$A = (20)^2$
$A = 314.159$ sq. ft.	$A = 400$ sq. ft.

Total area to fertilize = Lot area – (House + Driveway + Pool + Garden)
$$= 17{,}000 - (4{,}000 + 200 + 314.159 + 400)$$
$$= 12{,}085.841 \text{ sq ft}$$

Number of bags needed = Total area to fertilize ÷ 4,500 sq ft/bag = x

$$\frac{12{,}085.841}{4{,}500} = 2.68 \text{ bags}$$

Since we cannot purchase 2.68 bags we must purchase 3 full bags.
Total cost = Number of bags • $7.95
$$= 3 \bullet \$7.95$$
$$= \$23.85$$

Finding Volume and Surface Area of Common Three-Dimensional Figures:

- The **lateral area** is the area of the faces excluding the bases.
- The **surface area** is the total area of all the faces, including the bases.
- The **volume** is the number of cubic units in a solid.

Figure	Lateral Area	Surface Area	Volume
Right prism	Sum of areas of lateral faces (rectangles)	Lateral area plus 2 times the area of the base	Area of the base times height
Cube, side s	$4s^2$	$6s^2$	s^3
Right pyramid	Sum of areas of lateral faces (triangles)	Lateral area plus area of the base	(1/3) times the area of the base times the height

<u>Example:</u> Find the total surface area of the given figure.

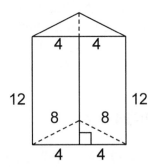

1. Since this is a triangular prism, first find the area of the bases.

2. Find the area of each rectangular lateral face.

3. Add the areas together.

The bases shown are equilateral triangles (all sides have length 8). To find the area of the base, we need the height of the base triangle. Use the Pythagorean Theorem.1.

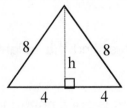

1. $A_{base} = \dfrac{1}{2}bh$

   $8^2 = 4^2 + h^2$ (to find the height of the base triangle)

   $h = 6.928$

   $A_{base} = \dfrac{1}{2}(8)(6.928) = 27.713$ sq units

2. $A_{face} = LW = (8)(12)$
   $= 96$ sq units

3. Total Area $= 2(27.713) + 3(96)$
   $= 343.426$ sq units

<u>Example:</u> A building shaped like a regular pyramid with a square base needs a fresh coat of paint. The painters will charge $5 per square foot. If the height of the building is 24 ft and each side of the square base is 20 ft, how much will it cost to paint the building?

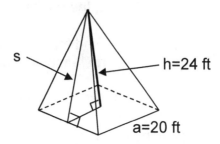

The painters will paint the lateral area of the pyramid. The lateral area is the sum of the areas of the four triangular faces.

In order to find the area of the triangle, we must first find the height of the triangle, which is the slant height of the pyramid.

Note in the figure that the slant height s is the hypotenuse of a right-angled triangle that has legs h (height of pyramid) and a/2 (half the length of the square base).

$$s = \sqrt{24^2 + 10^2} = \sqrt{576 + 100} = \sqrt{676} = 26 \text{ ft}$$

Area of one triangle = base x height/2 = 20 •26/2=260 sq ft
Lateral area of pyramid = 260 •4 = 1040 sq ft
Cost of painting the building = 1040 •5 = $5200.

Solids with circular bases have **area** and **volume** formulas that use the constant π.

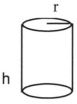

Right circular cylinder
Lateral Area = $2\pi rh$
Total Surface Area = $2\pi rh + 2\pi r^2 = 2\pi r(h + r)$ <small>(where r is the radius of the base)</small>
Volume = $\pi r^2 h$

Right circular cone
Lateral Area = πrs
Total Surface Area = $\pi rs + \pi r^2$
Volume = $\frac{1}{3}Bh = \frac{1}{3}(\pi r^2)h$

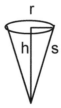

Sphere

Total Surface area = $4\pi r^2$

Volume = $\frac{4}{3}\pi r^3$

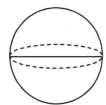

Example: How much material is needed to make a basketball that has a diameter of 15 inches? How much air is needed to fill the basketball?

Surface Area	Volume	
$SA = 4\pi r^2$	$V = \frac{4}{3}\pi r^3$	1. write formula
$= 4\pi(7.5)^2$	$= \frac{4}{3}\pi(7.5)^3$	2. substitute
material $= 706.858$ in^2	air $= 1767.1459$ in^3	3. solve

Skill 10.3   Determine how a change in dimensions (e.g., length, width, height, radius) affects other measurements (e.g., perimeter, area, surface area, volume)

Determining how a change in a dimension affects other measurements depends upon the role of the dimension in the formula.

If the formula involves addition, as in the case of the perimeter of a rectangle, examining the change in perimeter of a given figure requires first to find the existing perimeter given the original dimensions and then finding the new perimeter given the new dimensions.

If the formula involves multiplication, as in the case of area or volume, the change in the measurement is the same multiple as that of the multiple applied to the dimension. For example, if the radius of a circle is doubled, the circumference of the circle will be doubled.

Example: A circle has a radius of 5m. If the radius is doubled, by what factor will its circumference change?

Circumference C = $2\pi r$ where r is the radius.
Original circumference = $2\pi(5) = 10\pi$ m
Changed circumference = $2\pi(10) = 20\pi$ m

Thus the circumference is doubled when the radius is doubled.

If the dimension changed is raised to a power in the formula, the measurement will change by the multiple of the dimension raised to the same power. For example, consider the area of a circle.

Example: A circle has a radius of 4m. If its radius is doubled, by what factor will its area change?

Area of a circle $A = \pi r^2$ where r is the radius
Original area: $\pi r^2 = \pi(4)^2 = 16\pi$ sq.m.
Changed area: $\pi r^2 = \pi(8)^2 = 64\pi$ sq.m.

The radius has been doubled, but since the radius is squared, the overall effect is that the area is changed by 2^2.

Example: The side of a cube is 9 ft. in length. If each side of the cube is reduced to one-third of its initial length, by what factor will the surface area and volume of the cube change?

Surface area of a cube $= 6s^2$
Initial surface area $= 6 \cdot 9^2 = 486$
Changed surface area $= 6 \cdot 3^2 = 54$ sq ft, $(1/9)^{th}$ the initial

Volume of a cube $= a^3$ where a is the side of the cube.
Initial volume of cube $= 9 \cdot 9 \cdot 9 = 729$ cu ft
Changed volume of cube $= 3 \cdot 3 \cdot 3 = 27$ cu ft, $(1/27)^{th}$ the initial

When the side of the cube was reduced to one-third of its initial length, the surface area was reduced by a factor of 3^2 or 9 and the volume of the cube was reduced by a factor of 3^3 or 27.

Example: If the radius of a cylinder is doubled, by what factor will its volume change?

The volume of a cylinder is given by $V = \pi r^2 h$ where r is the radius of the cylinder and h is its height

If the radius of the cylinder is doubled, the ratio of the new and old volumes will be

$$\frac{V_{new}}{V_{old}} = \frac{\pi(2r)^2 h}{\pi r^2 h} = 4$$

Notice that the volume changes by a factor of 4 since the radius r is squared in the formula for the volume. The other length dimension h remains unchanged

Skill 10.4   Identify characteristics of three-dimensional figures (e.g., faces, edges, vertices)

A three-dimensional figure, sometimes called a solid, is composed of surface and plane regions, all within a three-dimensional space. The **faces** are the surface areas of the figure and are 2-dimensional. The **edges** are one-dimensional lines where the faces of the solid meet. The end points of the edges are called its **vertices** and are zero-dimensional.

The most common three-dimensional figures have only a few faces, the surfaces are very simple, and there are no "loose ends" - that is, every vertex is the end of at least two edges, and at least two faces meet at every edge.

The surfaces of a three-dimensional figure may be flat or curved. If all the faces are flat, every edge is the intersection of two faces, every vertex is the intersection of at least three edges, and no two faces cross each other, the figure is called a **polyhedron**. The fact that the faces are flat means that every edge is a straight line and every face is a polygon. A polyhedral is classified according to the number of faces (e.g. tetrahedron with 4 faces, octahedron with 8 faces).

Familiar polyhedra include **cubes**, **pyramids** and **rectangular or triangular prisms**. A cube has six identical square faces, 12 edges and 8 vertices.

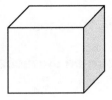

A pyramid is a polyhedron with three or more triangular faces meeting at a common vertex. The base is a polygon. The number of triangular faces is the same as the number of sides of the polygonal base. A pyramid with a triangular base is known as a **tetrahedron**. A square pyramid is shown below.

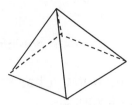

A prism is a polyhedron with two identical parallel faces known as bases. It is named according to the shape of the base and the shape of the base determines how many other faces the prism has. A triangular prism, for instance, has triangular bases and three faces (corresponding to the sides of the triangle) in addition to the bases.

For a polyhedron, the numbers of vertices (V), faces (F), and edges (E) are related by Euler's **Formula**: $V + F = E + 2$.

Example: We want to create a pentagonal pyramid, and we know it has six vertices and six faces. Using Euler's Formula, we compute:

$$V + F = E + 2$$
$$6 + 6 = E + 2$$
$$E = 10$$

Thus, we know that our figure should have 10 edges.

Common three-dimensional figures with **curved surfaces** include **spheres**, **cylinders** and **cones**.

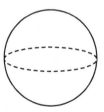

All points on the surface of a sphere are equidistant from its center.

A cylinder is similar to a prism in that it has two identical parallel bases. The bases, however, are circles and not polygons.

A cone is similar to a pyramid in that it has a single base and a vertex outside the base joined to every point on the perimeter of the base by a straight line. Here, again, the base is a circle and not a polygon.

Skill 10.5   Identify the net of a three-dimensional figure

A **net** is a two-dimensional figure that can be cut out and folded up to make a three-dimensional solid. Below are models of the five regular solids with their corresponding face polygons and nets.

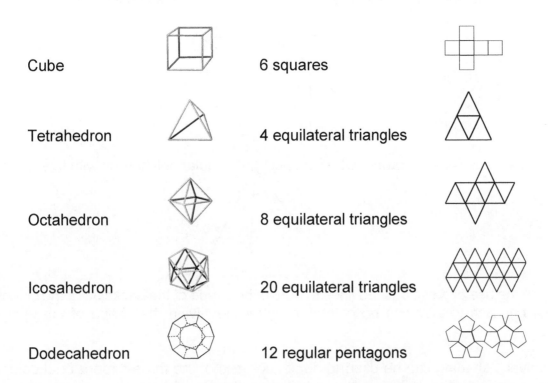

Cube	6 squares	
Tetrahedron	4 equilateral triangles	
Octahedron	8 equilateral triangles	
Icosahedron	20 equilateral triangles	
Dodecahedron	12 regular pentagons	

There can be more than one possible net for a particular three-dimensional figure. For instance, here are two more nets for a tetrahedron.

The following website has animations of unfolding polyhedra:
http://www.cs.mcgill.ca/~sqrt/unfold/unfolding.html

Skill 10.6   Identify the two-dimensional view of a three-dimensional figure

Since paper, computer screens and other such media are two-dimensional, the use of some special graphical effects is necessary to produce the illusion of a three-dimensional object. Understanding several crucial principles are helpful in identifying the two-dimensional view of a three dimensional object.

First, two-dimensional representations of three-dimensional objects often use dashed lines to represent the (invisible) back portion of the objects. This allows the viewer to know what the shape of the unseen portion is without significantly disturbing the picture.

Consider, for instance, a two-dimensional drawing of a cube, as shown below.

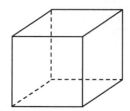

Another example is the following, which depicts an irregular polyhedron with five faces.

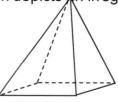

Although the use of these dashed lines to define the shape of the backside of the object are not necessary, they can be helpful in better identifying the shape of the entire object.

Alternatively, shading can be used to depict portions of the three-dimensional object that are only partially illuminated, thus creating an illusion of three dimensions.

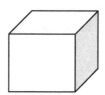

In the case of polyhedra, two-dimensional representations can be created by plotting (or drawing) the vertices and the edges. If the coordinates of the vertices are known, then these can be plotted using a basic set of three-dimensional axes, as shown below.

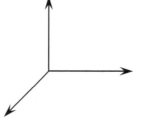

Points can be plotted by traversing the required distance parallel to each axis. Thus, the point (3, 3, 3) is plotted as shown below.

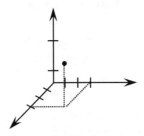

A cube with sides of length 2 can then be represented as shown below.

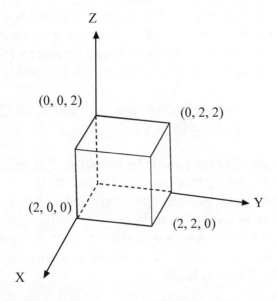

Thus, identifying the two-dimensional representation of a three-dimensional object requires knowledge of the basic shape of the object or the ability to plot (or draw) the object using three-dimensional coordinate axes.

Essential Tips for Every Math Teacher

Pedagogical principles and teaching methods are important for all teachers. They are particularly critical, though, for math teaching since math teachers not only face the difficulty of communicating the subject matter to students but also that of surmounting an all-pervasive cultural fear of mathematics. Math teachers need to take particular care to foster learning in a non-threatening environment that is at the same time genuinely stimulating and challenging.

The National Council of Teachers of Mathematics (NCTM) (http://www.nctm.org/) Principles and Standards emphasizes the teacher's obligation to support all students not only in developing basic mathematics knowledge and skills but also in their ability to understand and reason mathematically to solve problems relevant to today's world. The use of technology in the classroom is strongly advocated.

Resources for middle school teachers are available on the NCTM website at http://www.nctm.org/resources/middle.aspx.

The Drexel University Math Forum website provides the opportunity to interact with mentors and other math educators online. Some of the material on this website requires paid subscription but there are openly available archives as well. An overview of what the site provides is available at http://mathforum.org/about.forum.html. You may find the "Teacher2Teacher" service particularly useful; you can ask questions or browse the archives for a wealth of nitty-gritty everyday teaching information, suggestions and links to teaching tools.

Other instructional and professional development resources:
http://archives.math.utk.edu/k12.html
http://www.learnalberta.ca/Launch.aspx?content=/content/mesg/html/math6web/math6shell.html

Pedagogical Principles

Maintain a supportive, non-threatening environment

Many students unfortunately perceive mathematics as a threat. This becomes a particularly critical issue at the middle school level, where they learn algebra for the first time and are required to think in new ways. Since fear "freezes" the brain and makes thinking more difficult, a student's belief that he is no good at math becomes a self-fulfilling prophecy. A teacher's primary task in this situation is to foster a learning environment where every student feels that he or she can learn to think mathematically. Here are some ways to go about this:

Accept all comments and questions: Acknowledge all questions and comments that students make. If what the student says is inaccurate or irrelevant to the topic in hand, point that out gently but also show your understanding of the thought process that led to the comment. This will encourage students to speak up in class and enhance their learning.

Set aside time for group work: Assign activities to groups of students comprised of mixed ability levels. It is often easier for students to put forward their own thoughts as part of a friendly group discussion than when they are sitting alone at their desks with a worksheet. The more proficient students can help the less able ones and at the same time clarify their own thinking. You will essentially be using the advanced students in the class as a resource in a manner that also contributes to their own development. The struggling students will feel supported by their peers and not isolated from them.

Encourage classroom discussion of math topics: For instance, let the whole class share different ways in which they approach a certain problem. It will give you insight into your students' ways of thinking and make it easier to help them. It will allow even those who just listen to understand and correct errors in their thinking without being put on the spot.

Engage and challenge students

Maintaining a non-threatening environment should not mean dumbing down the math content in the classroom. The right level of challenge and relevance to their daily lives can help to keep students interested and learning. Here are some ideas:

Show connections to the real world: Use real life examples of math problems in your teaching. Some suggestions are given in the next section. Explain the importance of math literacy in society and the pitfalls of not being mathematically aware. An excellent reference is "The 10 Things All Future Mathematicians and Scientists Must Know" by Edward Zaccaro. The title of the book is misleading since it deals with things that every educated person, not just mathematicians and scientists, should know.

Use technology: Make use of calculators and computers including various online, interactive resources in your teaching. The natural affinity today's children have for these devices will definitely help them to engage more deeply in their math learning.

Demonstrate "messy" math: Children often have the mistaken belief that every math problem can be solved by following a particular set of rules; they either know the rules or they don't. In real life, however, math problems can be approached in different ways and often one has to negotiate several blind alleys before getting to the real solution. Children instinctively realize this while doing puzzles or playing games. They just don't associate this kind of thinking with classroom math. The most important insight any math teacher can convey to students is the realization that even if they don't know how to do a problem at first, they can think about it and figure it out as long as they are willing to stay with the problem and make mistakes in the process. An obvious way to do this, of course, is to introduce mathematical puzzles and games in the classroom. The best way, however, is for teachers themselves to take risks occasionally with unfamiliar problems and demonstrate to the class how one can work one's way out of a clueless state.

Show the reasoning behind rules: Even when it is not a required part of the curriculum, explain, whenever possible, how a mathematical rule is derived or how it is connected to other rules. For instance, in explaining the rule for finding the area of a trapezoid, show how one can get to it by thinking of the trapezoid as two triangles. This will reinforce the students' sense of mathematics as something that can be logically arrived at and not something for which they have to remember innumerable rules. Another way to reinforce this idea is to do the same problem using different approaches.

Be willing to take occasional side trips: Be flexible at times and go off topic in order to explore more deeply any questions or comments from the students. Grab a teaching opportunity even if it is irrelevant to the topic under discussion.

Help every student gain a firm grasp of fundamentals
While discussion, reasoning and divergent thinking is to be encouraged, it can only be done on a firm scaffolding of basic math knowledge. A firm grasp of math principles, for most people, does require rote exercises and doing more and more of the same type of problems. Just as practicing scales is essential for musical creativity, math creativity can only be built on a foundation strengthened by drilling and repetition. Many educators see independent reasoning and traditional rule-based drilling as opposing approaches. An effective teacher, however, must maintain a balance between the two and ensure that students have the basic tools they need to think independently.

Make sure all students actually know basic math rules and concepts: Test students regularly for basic math knowledge and provide reinforcement with additional practice wherever necessary.

Keep reviewing old material: Do not underestimate your students' ability to forget what they have not seen in a while. Link new topics whenever possible with things your students have learned before and take the opportunity to review previous learning. Most math textbooks nowadays have a spiral review section created with this end in mind.

<u>Keep mental math muscles strong:</u> The calculator, without question, is a very valuable learning tool. Many students, unfortunately, use it as a crutch to the point that they lose the natural feel for numbers and ability to estimate that people develop through mental calculations. As a result, they are often unable to tell when they punch a wrong button and get a very unreasonable answer. Take your students through frequent mental calculation exercises; you can easily integrate it into class discussions. Teach them useful strategies for making mental estimates.

Specific Teaching Methods
Some commonly used teaching techniques and tools are described below along with links to further information. The links provided in the first part of this chapter also provide a wealth of instructional ideas and material.

A very useful resource is the book "Family Math: The Middle School Years" from the Lawrence Hall of Science, University of California at Berkeley. Although this book was developed for use by families, teachers in school can choose from the many simple activities and games used to reinforce two significant middle school skills, algebraic reasoning and number sense. A further advantage is that all the activities are based on NCTM standards. Each activity lists the specific math concepts that are covered.

Here are some tools you can use to make your teaching more effective:

Classroom openers
To start your class with stimulated, interested and focused students, provide a short opening activity every day. You can make use of thought-provoking questions, puzzles or tricks. Use relevant puzzles or tricks to illustrate specific topics at any point in your class. The following website provides some ideas:
http://mathforum.org/k12/k12puzzles/

Real life examples
Connect math to other aspects of your students' lives by using examples and data from the real world whenever possible. It will not only keep them engaged, it will also help answer the perennial question "Why do we have to learn math?"

Online resources to get you started:

1. Election math in the classroom:
   http://mathforum.org/t2t/faq/election.html

2. Math worksheets related to the Iditarod, an annual Alaskan sled dog race:
   http://www.educationworld.com/a_lesson/lesson/lesson302.shtml

Manipulatives

Manipulatives can help all students learn; particularly those oriented more towards visual and kinesthetic learning. Here are some ideas for the use of manipulatives in the classroom:

1. Use tiles, pattern blocks or geoboards to demonstrate geometry concepts such as shapes, area and perimeter. In the example shown below, 12 tiles are used to form different rectangles.

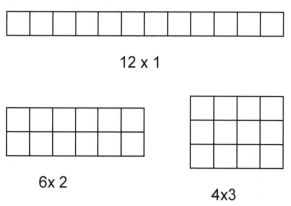

12 x 1

6x 2

4x3

2. Stacks of blocks representing numbers are useful for teaching basic statistics concepts such as mean, median and mode. Rearranging the blocks to make each stack the same height would demonstrate the mean or average value of the data set. The example below shows a data set represented by stacks of blocks. Rearranging the blocks to make the height of each stack equal to three shows that this is the mean value.

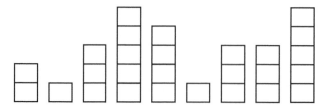

3. Tiles, blocks, or other countable manipulatives such as beans can also be used to demonstrate numbers in different bases. Each stack will represent a place with the number of blocks in the stack showing the place value.

4. Playing cards can be used for a discussion of probability.

5. Addition and subtraction of integers, positive and negative, is a major stumbling block for many middle school students. Two sets of tiles, marked with pluses and minuses respectively, can be used to demonstrate these concepts visually with each "plus" tile canceling a "minus" tile.

   A practical demonstration of percent changes can be made by photocopying a figure using different copier magnifications.

6. Algeblocks are blocks designed specifically for the teaching of algebra with manipulatives   http://www.hand2mind.com/category/math/algebra/3009

7. Software

Spreadsheets can be very effective math learning tools. Here are some ideas for using spreadsheets in the classroom:
http://www.angelfire.com/wi2/spreadsheet/necc.html

Word problem strategies
Word problems, a challenge for many students even in elementary school, become more complicated and sometimes intimidating in the middle grades. Here are some ideas students can use to tackle them:

1. Identify significant words and numbers in the problem. Highlight or underline them. If necessary, write them in the form of a table.

2. Draw diagrams to clarify the problem. Put down the main items or events and numbers on the diagram and show the relationships between them.

3. Rewrite the problem using fewer and simpler words. One way is to have a standard format for this as shown in the example below.

   Problem: Calculate the cost of 3 pencils given that 5 pencils cost 25 cents.
   Rewrite as:
   Cost of 5 pencils = 25 cents
   Cost of 1 pencil = 25/5 = 5 cents
   Cost of 3 pencils = 5 X 3 = 15 cents

4. If you have no idea how to approach the problem, try the guess and check approach at first. That will give you a sense of the kind of problem you are dealing with.

5. Create similar word problems of your own.

Equation rule

Solving algebraic equations is a challenge for many learners particularly when they think they need to remember many different rules. Emphasize the fact that they only need to keep only one rule in mind whether they are adding, subtracting, multiplying or dividing numbers or variables:

"Do the same thing to both sides"

A balance or teeter-totter metaphor can help to clarify their understanding of equations. You can also use manipulatives to demonstrate.

Mental math practice

Give students regular practice in doing mental math. The following website offers many mental calculation tips and strategies:
http://mathforum.org/k12/mathtips/mathtips.html

Because frequent calculator use tends to deprive students of a sense of numbers, they will often approach a sequence of multiplications and divisions the hard way. For instance, asked to calculate 770 x 36/ 55, they will first multiply 770 and 36 and then do a long division with the 55. They fail to recognize that both 770 and 55 can be divided by 11 and then by 5 to considerably simplify the problem. Give students plenty of practice in multiplying and dividing a sequence of integers and fractions so they are comfortable with canceling top and bottom terms.

Math language

There is an explosion of new math words as students enter the middle grades and start learning algebra and geometry.

This website provides an animated, colorfully illustrated dictionary of math terms:
http://www.amathsdictionaryforkids.com/

WEB LINKS

ALGEBRA

Algebra
Different levels plus quiz
- http://www.math.com/homeworkhelp/Algebra.html

Algebraic Structures
Symbols and sets of numbers
- http://www.wtamu.edu/academic/anns/mps/math/mathlab/beg_algebra/beg_alg_tut2_sets.htm
Integers
- http://amby.com/educate/math/integer.html
Card game to add and subtract integers
- http://www.education-world.com/a_tsl/archives/03-1/lesson001.shtml
Multiplying integers
- http://www.aaastudy.com/mul65_x2.htm

Polynomial Equations and Inequalities
Inequality tutorial, examples, problems
- http://www.wtamu.edu/academic/anns/mps/math/mathlab/beg_algebra/beg_alg_tut18_ineq.htm
Graphing linear inequalities tutorial
- http://www.wtamu.edu/academic/anns/mps/math/mathlab/beg_algebra/beg_alg_tut24_ineq.htm
Quadratic equations tutorial, examples, problems
- http://www.wtamu.edu/academic/anns/mps/math/mathlab/col_algebra/col_alg_tut17_quad.htm
Synthetic division tutorial:
- http://www.wtamu.edu/academic/anns/mps/math/mathlab/col_algebra/col_alg_tut37_syndiv.htm
Synthetic division Examples and problems
- http://www.tpub.com/math1/10h.htm

Functions
Function, domain, range intro and practice
- http://www.mathwarehouse.com/algebra/relation/math-function.php
Equations with rational expressions tutorial
- http://www.wtamu.edu/academic/anns/mps/math/mathlab/col_algebra/col_alg_tut15_rateq.htm
Radical equations – lesson and practice
- http://regentsprep.org/REgents/mathb/mathb-topic.cfm?TopicCode=7D3
Logarithmic functions tutorial
- http://www.wtamu.edu/academic/anns/mps/math/mathlab/col_algebra/col_alg_tut43_logfun.htm

Linear Algebra
Vector practice tip
- http://www.phy.mtu.edu/~suits/PH2100/vecdot.html

GEOMETRY

Geometry
- http://www.math.com/students/homeworkhelp.html#geometry

Parallelism
Parallel lines practice
- http://www.algebralab.org/lessons/lesson.aspx?file=Geometry_AnglesParallel LinesTransversals.xml

Plane Euclidean Geometry
- http://www.mathwarehouse.com/geometry/
Triangles intro and practice
- http://www.staff.vu.edu.au/mcaonline/units/geometry/triangles.html
Interactive parabola
- http://www.mathwarehouse.com/geometry/parabola/
Ellipse practice problems
- http://www.mathwarehouse.com/ellipse/equation-of-ellipse.php#equationOfEllipse

Transformational Geometry
Interactive transformational geometry practice on coordinate plane
- http://www.shodor.org/interactivate/activities/Transmographer/
Similar triangles practice
- http://www.algebralab.org/practice/practice.aspx?file=Geometry_UsingSimilar Triangles.xml

NUMBER THEORY
Natural Numbers
- http://online.math.uh.edu/MiddleSchool/Vocabulary/NumberTheoryVocab.pdf

PROBABILITY AND STATISTICS

Probability
Probability intro and practice
- http://www.mathgoodies.com/lessons/vol6/intro_probability.html

Statistics

Statistics lessons and interactive practice
- http://aaaknow.com/toc.php?menu=Statistics

Range, mean, median, mode exercises
- http://www.mathgoodies.com/lessons/toc_vol8.html

SAMPLE TEST

DIRECTIONS: Read each item and select the best response.

1. **What would be the total cost of a suit for $295.99 and a pair of shoes for $69.95 including 6.5% sales tax?** *(Average)(Skill 1.1)*

   A) $389.73

   B) $398.37

   C) $237.86

   D) $315.23

2. **What is the smallest number that is divisible by 3 and 5 and leaves a remainder of 3 when divided by 7?** *(Average) (Skill 1.2)*

   A) 15

   B) 18

   C) 25

   D) 45

3. **When considering a reasonable prediction for the outcome of the expression $6^2 - 4(5)(-10)$, a student should be able to expect that:** *(Average)(Skill 1.3)*

   A) The answer will be zero

   B) The answer will be positive

   C) The answer will be an odd number

   D) A calculator must be used to finish the problem.

4. **A student had 60 days to appeal the results of an exam. If the results were received on March 23, what was the last day that the student could appeal?** *(Average)(Skill 1.4)*

   A) May 21

   B) May 22

   C) May 23

   D) May 24

5. Which of the following is always composite if *x* is odd, *y* is even, and both *x* and *y* are greater than or equal to 2?
   (Rigorous) (Skill 1.5)

   A) $x + y$

   B) $3x + 2y$

   C) $5xy$

   D) $5x + 3y$

6. What can be deduced from the following statements?
   (Average Rigor) (Skill 1.6)
   - **All Saint Bernards are dogs**
   - **If an animal is a dog, then it has 4 legs.**

   A) All Saint Bernards rescue skiers.

   B) All 4-legged animals are dogs.

   C) Saint Bernards have 4 legs.

   D) A dog is an animal.

7. Which is the least appropriate strategy to emphasize when teaching problem solving?
   (Easy)(Skill 1.7)

   A) guess and check

   B) look for key words to indicate operations such as all together—add, more than, subtract, times, multiply

   C) make a diagram

   D) solve a simpler version of the problem

8. When you begin by assuming the conclusion of a theorem is false, then show that through a sequence of logically correct steps you contradict an accepted fact, this is known as
   (Easy)(Skill 1.8)

   A) inductive reasoning

   B) direct proof

   C) indirect proof

   D) exhaustive proof

9. The diagram below would be least appropriate for illustrating which of the following? *(Average)(Skill 2.1)*

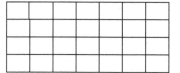

A) $7 \times 4 + 3$

B) $31 \div 8$

C) 28×3

D) $31 - 3$

10. Which of the choices below does not represent a reasonable conclusion made from the Venn diagram? *(Average) (Skill 2.2)*

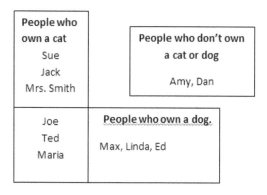

A) Amy has a fish

B) Mrs. Smith has a cat.

C) 3 people have a dog and a cat.

D) 6 people have a dog.

11. Choose the least appropriate set of manipulatives for a sixth grade class. *(Easy)(Skill 2.3)*

A) graphing calculators, compasses, rulers, conic section models

B) two color counters, origami paper, markers, yarn

C) balance, meter stick, colored pencils, beads

D) paper cups, beans, tangrams, geoboards

12. Which of the following is not an example of Assistive Technology? *(Average) (Skill 2.4)*

A) A worksheet that has been enlarged on a copy machine.

B) A teacher microphone linked to a student speaker

C) A closed circuit monitor displaying the teacher

D) A set of place value blocks

13. A unit test covering three weeks of class material is best described as which kind of assessment? *(Easy) (Skill 3.1)*

A) Final

B) Formative

C) Summative

D) Directive

14. Which of the following describe a technique that a teacher should use when analyzing student work and performance in order to improve student learning? *(Rigorous) (Skill 3.2)*

A) Have a clear understanding of the student objectives

B) Assess work according to set standards or rubrics

C) Reflect on the overall class performance

D) All of the above

15. Which choice below shows the best example of how a teacher can use technology to efficiently analyze student performance? *(Average) (Skill 3.3)*

A) Use an audience response system as part of the lesson.

B) Have students raise their hands in response to a question.

C) Tell students which numbers to type into their calculators.

D) Have students type an equation into a graphing calculator.

16. If a class performs poorly on a test, the teacher should *(Average) (Skill 3.4)*

A) Make an easier test.

B) Review results to see which items were most frequently missed and re-teach those concepts.

C) Not count the test toward the students' grades.

D) Re-teach the entire unit.

17. In order to question a student at a high level of cognitive complexity, *(Average) (Skill 3.5)*

A) The teacher should ask questions about material that will be taught next year.

B) The problem should use numbers with at least three digits.

C) The question should integrate a need for processing skills and a series of multiple steps to reach the solution.

D) The teacher should ask the question from the front of the room.

18. Higher order thinking, creativity, and the integration of reasoning and communication skills are most demonstrated by *(Easy) (Skill 3.6)*

    A) Multiple-choice and true/false tests

    B) Projects, demonstrations and oral presentations

    C) Essay questions

    D) Portfolios

19. When a math student returns from an absence, they should be encouraged to *(Easy) (Skill 4.1)*

    A) Not worry about the work that was missed

    B) Wait until the end of the chapter to complete any missed work

    C) Copy another student's homework

    D) Spend extra time completing any missed work as soon as possible.

20. The phrase "two negatives make a positive" can cause a misconception when considering *(Average) (Skill 4.2)*

    A) The negative portions of the *x* and *y*-axes on the coordinate plane

    B) The addition of two negative numbers versus the multiplication of two negative.

    C) Imaginary numbers

    D) none of the above

21. Which of the following is not true about multiplication? *(Easy) (Skill 4.3)*

    A) Multiplication is only used in Algebra

    B) Multiplication represents repeated addition

    C) Multiplication is Commutative and Associative

    D) Multiplication can be modeled with area diagrams

22. A student turns in a paper with this type of error:

$7 + 16 \div 8 \times 2 = 8$

$8 - 3 \times 3 + 4 = -5$

(Rigorous)(Skill 4.4)

In order to remediate this error, a teacher should:

A) review and drill basic number facts

B) emphasize the importance of using parentheses in simplifying expressions

C) emphasize the importance of working from left to right when applying the order of operations

D) do nothing; these answers are correct

23. **Which of the following is a middle school mathematics skill that is needed for higher levels of math?** *(Average) (Skill 4.5)*

A) Number sense

B) Recognizing patterns

C) Knowing properties of Geometric shapes

D) All of the above

24. **Choose the set in which the members are not equivalent.** *(Average)(Skill 5.1)*

A) 1/2, 0.5, 50%

B) 10/5, 2.0, 200%

C) 3/8, 0.385, 38.5%

D) 7/10, 0.7, 70%

25. **When modeling the addition of the following numbers by hand: (-1) + 14 + 3 + 2 +18 +(-3) + 7, the teacher should** *(Average) (Skill 5.2)*

A) Round each value up

B) Add all the negatives together first, then the positives

C) First combine opposites, then add numbers that make sets of 10.

D) Add the numbers up from left to right, then from right to left, and be sure the answers match.

26. Which of the following is not true about the prime factorization of every composite number? *(Rigorous) (Skill 5.3)*

   A) The prime factorization will contain exponents

   B) The prime factorization can be used in simplifying expressions

   C) The prime factorization consists of prime numbers

   D) The prime factorization is unique.

27. Find the GCF of $2^2 \cdot 3^2 \cdot 5$ and $2^2 \cdot 3 \cdot 7$. *(Average)(Skill 5.4)*

   A) $2^5 \cdot 3^3 \cdot 5 \cdot 7$

   B) $2 \cdot 3 \cdot 5 \cdot 7$

   C) $2 \cdot 3$

   D) $2^3 \cdot 3^2 \cdot 5 \cdot 7$

28. If three cups of concentrate are needed to make 2 gallons of fruit punch, how many cups are needed to make 5 gallons? *(Easy)(Skill 5.5)*

   A) 6 cups

   B) 7 cups

   C) 7.5 cups

   D) 10 cups

29. Sandra has $34.00, Carl has $42.00. Which would be the best method for determining how much more money Carl has than Sandra? *(Easy)(Skill 5.6)*

   A) addition

   B) subtraction

   C) division

   D) both A and B are equally correct

30. {1,4,7,10, . . .} What is the 40th term in this sequence? *(Rigorous)(Skill 6.1)*

   A) 43

   B) 121

   C) 118

   D) 120

31. Which set illustrates a function? *(Easy)(Skill 6.2)*

   A) { (0,1) (0,2) (0,3) (0,4) }

   B) { (3,9) (−3,9) (4,16) (− 4,16) }

   C) { (1,2) (2,3) (3,4) (1,4) }

   D) { (2,4) (3,6) (4,8) (4,16) }

32. Combine and simplify: $\sqrt{75} + \sqrt{147} - \sqrt{48}$
   (Rigorous)(Skill 6.3)

   A) 174

   B) $12\sqrt{3}$

   C) $8\sqrt{3}$

   D) 74

33. Evaluate $3^{1/2}(9^{1/3})$
   (Rigorous)(Skill 6.4)

   A) $27^{5/6}$

   B) $9^{7/12}$

   C) $3^{5/6}$

   D) $3^{6/7}$

34. Solve for x: $3x + 5 \geq 8 + 7x$
   (Average)(Skill 6.5)

   A) $x \geq -\frac{3}{4}$

   B) $x \leq -\frac{3}{4}$

   C) $x \geq \frac{3}{4}$

   D) $x \leq \frac{3}{4}$

35. Solve for x: $|2x + 3| > 4$
   (Rigorous)(Skill 6.5)

   A) $-\frac{7}{2} > x > \frac{1}{2}$

   B) $-\frac{1}{2} > x > \frac{7}{2}$

   C) $x < \frac{7}{2}$ or $x < -\frac{1}{2}$

   D) $x < -\frac{7}{2}$ or $x > \frac{1}{2}$

36. Which graph represents the solution set for $x^2 + 6 > 5x$?
   (Rigorous) (Skill 6.6)

   A)
         -2 0 2

   B)
         -3 0 3

   C)
         -2 0 2

   D)
         -3 0 2 3

37. Identify the proper sequencing of subskills when teaching graphing inequalities in two dimensions *(Easy)(Skill 6.7)*

   A) shading regions, graphing lines, graphing points, determining whether a line is solid or broken

   B) graphing points, graphing lines, determining whether a line is solid or broken, shading regions

   C) graphing points, shading regions, determining whether a line is solid or broken, graphing lines

   D) graphing lines, determining whether a line is solid or broken, graphing points, shading regions

38. A burning candle loses ½ inch in height every hour. If the original height of the candle was 6 inches, which of the following equations describes the relationship between the height h of the candle and the number of hours t since it was lit? *(Rigorous)(Skill 6.8)*

   A) 2h + t = 12

   B) 2h – t = 12

   C) h = 6 - t

   D) h = 0.5t + 6

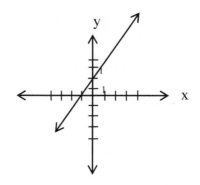

39. What is the equation of the above graph? *(Rigorous)(Skill 6.9)*

   A) $2x + y = 2$

   B) $2x - y = -2$

   C) $2x - y = 2$

   D) $2x + y = -2$

40. Put the following numbers in order from least to greatest. *(Average)(Skill 6.10)*

   $12.2,\ 0,\ 7,\ \sqrt{14},\ \sqrt{25},\ \sqrt{\frac{1}{4}},\ 3 \times 10^{-4}$

   A) $12.2,\ 0,\ 7,\ \sqrt{14},\ \sqrt{25},\ \sqrt{\frac{1}{4}},\ 3 \times 10^{-4}$

   B) $3 \times 10^{-4},\ 0,\ 7,\ 12.2,\ \sqrt{14},\ \sqrt{25},\ \sqrt{\frac{1}{4}}$

   C) $0,\ \sqrt{\frac{1}{4}},\ 7,\ 12.2,\ \sqrt{14},\ \sqrt{25},\ 3 \times 10^{-4}$

   D) $0,\ 3 \times 10^{-4},\ \sqrt{\frac{1}{4}},\ \sqrt{14},\ \sqrt{25},\ 7, 12.2$

41. Which statement is an example of the additive identity?
(Easy)(Skill 6.11)

A) 3 + –3 = 0

B) 3x = 3x + 0

C) $3 \cdot \dfrac{1}{3} = 1$

D) 3 + 2x = 2x + 3

42. Given a graph for a function f(x) describe how the graph of –f(x) will compare to the original.
(Easy) (Skill 7.1)

A) Flipped over the x axis

B) Flipped over the y axis

C) Rotated 90°

D) Unchanged

43. .What is the slope of any line parallel to the line 2x + 4y = 4?
(Rigorous)(Skill 7.2)

A) -2

B) -1

C) – ½

D) 2

44. Factor completely:
8(x – y) + a(y – x)
(Rigorous)(Skill 7.3)

A) (8 + a)(y – x)

B) (8 – a)(y – x)

C) (a – 8)(y – x)

D) (a – 8)(y + x)

45. Find the zeroes of
$f(x) = x^3 + x^2 - 14x - 24$
(Rigorous)(Skill 7.3)

A) 4, 3, 2

B) 3, –8

C) 7, –2, –1

D) 4, –3, –2

46. Solve for x and y: x= 3y + 7, 7x + 5y = 23 *(Rigorous)(Skill 7.4)*

A) (–1,4)

B) (4, –1)

C) $(\frac{-29}{7}, \frac{-26}{7})$

D) (10, 1)

47. Which graph shows the solution to the system of inequalities below? *(Rigorous) (Skill 7.5)*

$3x - 2y \leq 5$
$-x + 5y > 1$

A)

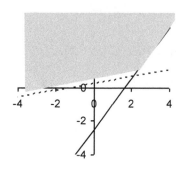

B)

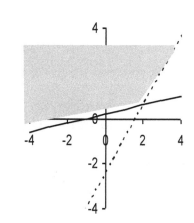

C)

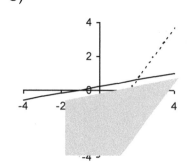

D)

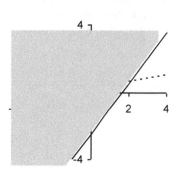

48. Solve for x.
$3x^2 - 2 + 4(x^2 - 3) = 0$
(Rigorous)(Skill 7.6)

A) $\{ -\sqrt{2}, \sqrt{2} \}$

B) $\{ 2, -2 \}$

C) $\{ 0, \sqrt{3}, -\sqrt{3} \}$

D) $\{ 7, -7 \}$

49. Which equation is graphed?

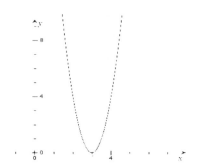

(Rigorous)(Skill 7.7)

A) $y = 4 (x + 3)^2$

B) $y = 4 (x - 3)^2$

C) $y = 3 (x - 4)^2$

D) $y = 3 (x + 4)^2$

50. Solve for x: $\sqrt{3 - 2x} = 7$
    (Average) (Skill 7.8)

    A) -23

    B) -2

    C) 5

    D) no solution

51. 2^{-3} is equivalent
    to *(Average)(Skill 7.9)*

    A) 0.8

    B) −0.8

    C) 125

    D) 0.125

52. Which of the following is
    incorrect? *(Rigorous)(Skill 7.9)*

    A) $(x^2 y^3)^2 = x^4 y^6$

    B) $m^2 (2n)^3 = 8m^2 n^3$

    C) $(m^3 n^4)/(m^2 n^2) = mn^2$

    D) $(x + y^2)^2 = x^2 + y^4$

53. Compute the median for the
    following data set:
    {12, 19, 13, 16, 17, 14}
    (Average)(Skill 8.1)

    A) 14.5

    B) 15.17

    C) 15

    D) 16

54. Corporate salaries are listed for
    several employees. Which best
    describes the range of the data?
    (Average)(Skill 8.2)

    $24,000 $24,000 $26,000
    $28,000 $30,000 $120,000

    A) $96,000

    B.) $120,000

    C) $120,000 - $24,000

    D) no range

55. What conclusion can be drawn
    from the graph below?
    (Average)(Skill 8.3)

    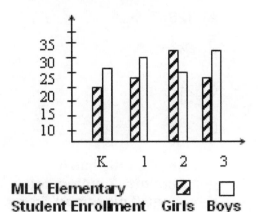

    MLK Elementary
    Student Enrollment   Girls   Boys

    A) The number of students in first
       grade exceeds the number in
       second grade.

    B) There are more boys than girls
       in the entire school.

    C) There are more girls than boys
       in the first grade.

    D) Third grade has the largest
       number of students.

56. Which of the following types of graphs would be best to use to record the eye color of the students in the class? *(Average) (Skill 8.4)*

A) Bar graph or circle graph

B) Pictograph or bar graph

C) Line graph or pictograph

D) Line graph or bar graph

57. How many ways are there to choose a potato and two green vegetables from a choice of three potatoes and seven green vegetables? *(Rigorous)(Skill 8.5)*

A) 126

B) 63

C) 21

D) 252

58. A sack of candy has 3 peppermints, 2 butterscotch drops and 3 cinnamon drops. One candy is drawn and replaced, then another candy is drawn; what is the probability that both will be butterscotch? *(Average)(Skill 8.6)*

A) 1/2

B) 1/28

C) 1/4

D) 1/16

59. Which of the following is a correct name for the ray? *(Easy) (Skill 9.1)*

A) $\overrightarrow{PU}$

B) $\overrightarrow{PT}$

C) $\overrightarrow{UT}$

D) Both A and B

60. Given $l_1 \parallel l_2$ which of the following is true? *(Average)(Skill 9.2)*

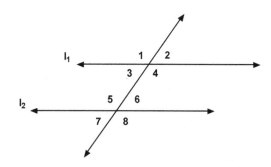

A) ∠1 and ∠8 are congruent and alternate interior angles

B) ∠2 and ∠3 are congruent and corresponding angles

C) ∠3 and ∠4 are adjacent and supplementary angles

D) ∠3 and ∠5 are adjacent and supplementary angles

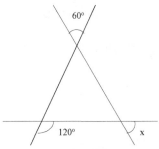

Note: Figure not drawn to scale.

61. In the figure above, what is the value of x? *(Rigorous)(Skill 9.3)*

A) 50°

B) 60°

C) 75°

D) 80°

62. What is the degree measure of an interior angle of a regular 10-sided polygon? *(Rigorous)(Skill 9.3)*

A) 18°

B) 36°

C) 144°

D) 54°

63. Given △DOG is isosceles with $\overline{DO} \cong \overline{OG}$ and m<O = 22°, find m<D. *(Easy)(Skill 9.4)*

A) 180°

B) 158°

C) 79°

D) none of the above

64. Given any △ABC, which of the following statements might not be true? *(Rigorous)(Skill 9.5)*

A) m<A + m<B + m<C = 180°

B) a + b >c

C) b + c >a

D) $a^2 + b^2 = c^2$

65. Which theorem can be used to prove $\triangle BAK \cong \triangle MKA$? *(Rigorous)(Skill 9.6)*

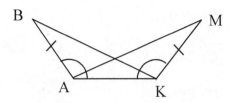

A) SSS

B) ASA

C) SAS

D) AAS

66. Ginny and Nick head back to their respective colleges after being home for the weekend. They leave their house at the same time and drive for 4 hours. Ginny drives due south at the average rate of 60 miles per hour and Nick drives due east at the average rate of 60 miles per hour. What is the straight-line distance between them, in miles, at the end of the 4 hours? *(Rigorous)(Skill 9.7)*

A) $120\sqrt{2}$

B) 240

C) $240\sqrt{2}$

D) 288

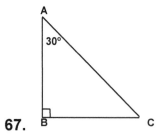

67.

If AC = 12, determine BC. *(Average)(Skill 9.7)*

A) 6

B) 4

C) $6\sqrt{3}$

D) $3\sqrt{6}$

68. Determine the measures of angles A and B. *(Average) (Skill 9.8)*

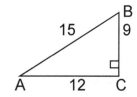

A) A = 30°, B = 60°

B) A = 60°, B = 30°

C) A = 53°, B = 37°

D) A = 37°, B = 53°

69. Which of the following is true about a parallelogram? *(Average)(Skill 9.9)*

A) The opposite sides are congruent.

B) The diagonals are congruent.

C) All four angles are congruent.

D) The sum of the interior angles is 180°.

70. Given segment AC with B as its midpoint find the coordinates of C if A = (5, 7) and B = (3, 6.5). *(Rigorous)(Skill 9.10)*

A) (4, 6.5)

B) (1, 6)

C) (2, 0.5)

D) (16, 1)

71. Find the distance between (3,7) and (–3,4). *(Average)(Skill 9.10)*

    A) 9

    B) 45

    C) $3\sqrt{5}$

    D) $5\sqrt{3}$

72. In similar polygons, if the perimeters are in a ratio of x : y, the sides are in a ratio of *(Rigorous)(Skill 9.11)*

    A) x : y

    B) $x^2 : y^2$

    C) 2x : y

    D) 1/2 x : y

73. If a circle has an area of 25 cm², what is its circumference to the nearest tenth of a centimeter? *(Rigorous)(Skill 9.12)*

    A) 78.5 cm

    B) 17.7 cm

    C) 8.9 cm

    D) 15.7 cm

74. 4 square yards is equivalent to *(Average)(Skill 10.1)*

    A) 12 square feet

    B) 48 square feet

    C) 36 square feet

    D) 108 square feet

75. Find the area of the figure below. *(Rigorous)(Skill 10.2)*

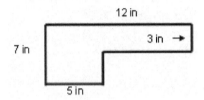

    A) 56 in²

    B) 27 in²

    C) 71 in²

    D) 170 in²

76. Determine the volume of a sphere to the nearest cm if the surface area is 113 cm². *(Rigorous)(Skill 10.2)*

    A) 113 cm³

    B) 339 cm³

    C) 37.7 cm³

    D) 226 cm3

77. If the radius of a right circular cylinder is doubled, how does its volume change? *(Rigorous)(Skills 10.3)*

   A) no change

   B) also is doubled

   C) four times the original

   D) pi times the original

78. A figure with 6 faces can be *(Easy)(Skill 10.4)*

   A) a hexagon

   B) a cylinder

   C) a sphere

   D) a cube

79. Giving students a worksheet with a pattern to color, cut out, and fold into a tetrahedron would be *(Rigorous) (Skill 10.5)*

   A) A way for students to work with the net of a three-dimensional figure

   B) An opportunity for students to learn how to share craft supplies.

   C) A proof of congruent triangles.

   D) An example of the Commutative Property of Addition.

80. Which of the following techniques or features can be used when drawing a 3-D figure on a piece of paper? *(Average)(Skill 10.6)*

   A) shading

   B) dotted lines

   C) a set of 3-D coordinate axes

   D) all of the above

ANSWER KEY

1. A		41. B	
2. D		42. A	
3. B		43. C	
4. B		44. C	
5. C		45. D	
6. C		46. B	
7. B		47. A	
8. C		48. A	
9. C		49. B	
10. A		50. A	
11. A		51. D	
12. D		52. D	
13. C		53. C	
14. D		54. A	
15. A		55. B	
16. B		56. B	
17. C		57. B	
18. B		58. D	
19. D		59. D	
20. B		60. C	
21. A		61. B	
22. C		62. C	
23. D		63. C	
24. C		64. D	
25. C		65. C	
26. A		66. C	
27. C		67. A	
28. C		68. D	
29. B		69. A	
30. C		70. B	
31. B		71. C	
32. C		72. A	
33. B		73. B	
34. B		74. C	
35. D		75. A	
36. D		76. A	
37. B		77. C	
38. A		78. D	
39. B		79. A	
40. D		80. D	

Rigor Table

	Easy 20%	Average 40 %	Rigorous 40%
Questions	7, 8, 11, 13, 18, 19, 21, 28, 29, 31, 37, 41, 42, 59, 63, 78	1, 2, 3, 4, 6, 9, 10, 12, 15, 16,17, 20, 23, 24, 25, 27, 34, 40, 50, 51, 53, 54, 55, 56, 58, 60, 67, 68, 69, 71, 74, 80	5, 14, 22, 26, 30, 32, 33, 35, 36, 38, 39, 43, 44, 45, 46, 47, 48, 49, 52, 57, 61, 62, 64, 65, 66, 70, 72, 73, 75, 76, 77, 79

RATIONALES WITH SAMPLE QUESTIONS

The following represent one way to solve the problems and obtain a correct answer. There are many other mathematically correct ways of determining the correct answer.

1. **What would be the total cost of a suit for $295.99 and a pair of shoes for $69.95 including 6.5% sales tax?** *(Average)(Skill 1.1)*

   A) $389.73
   B) $398.37
   C) $237.86
   D) $315.23

The correct answer is A.
Before the tax, the total comes to $365.94. Then .065($365.94) = $23.79. With the tax added on, the total bill is $365.94 + $23.79 = $389.73. (Quicker way: 1.065($365.94) = $389.73.)

2. **What is the smallest number that is divisible by 3 and 5 and leaves a remainder of 3 when divided by 7?** *(Average) (Skill 1.2)*

   A) 15
   B) 18
   C) 25
   D) 45

The correct answer is D.
To be divisible by both 3 and 5, the number must be divisible by 15. Inspecting the first few multiples of 15, you will find that 45 is the first of the sequence that is 4 3 greater than a multiple of 7.

3. **When considering a reasonable prediction for the outcome of the expression $6^2 - 4(5)(-10)$, a student should be able to expect that:** *(Average)(Skill 1.3)*

   A) The answer will be zero
   B) The answer will be positive
   C) The answer will be an odd number
   D) A calculator must be used to finish the problem.

The correct answer is B.
In order to avoid any errors in calculation, it is helpful to notice that the (-4) multiplied with the (-10) will result in a positive product, thereby making a positive answer to the problem.

4. **A student had 60 days to appeal the results of an exam. If the results were received on March 23, what was the last day that the student could appeal?** *(Average)(Skill 1.4)*

   A) May 21
   B) May 22
   C) May 23
   D) May 24

The correct answer is B.
Recall: 30 days in April and 31 in March. 8 days in March + 30 days in April + 22 days in May brings him to a total of 60 days on May 22. Answer is B.

5. **Which of the following is always composite if *x* is odd, *y* is even, and both *x* and *y* are greater than or equal to 2?** *(Rigorous) (Skill 1.5)*

   A) $x+y$
   B) $3x+2y$
   C) $5xy$
   D) $5x+3y$

The correct answer is C.
A composite number is a number, which is not prime. The prime number sequence begins 2,3,5,7,11,13,17, …To determine which of the expressions is <u>always</u> composite, experiment with different values of *x* and *y*, such as *x*=3 and *y*=2, or *x*=5 and *y*=2. It turns out that 5*xy* will always be an even number, and therefore, composite.

6. **What can be deduced from the following statements?**
   - **All Saint Bernards are dogs**
   - **If an animal is a dog, then it has 4 legs.**
   (Average) (Skill 1.6)

   A) All Saint Bernards rescue skiers.
   B) All 4 legged animals are dogs.
   C) Saint Bernards have 4 legs.
   D) A dog is an animal.

The correct answer is C.
Statement C is the logical deduction that can be made from the above statements.

7. **Which is the least appropriate strategy to emphasize when teaching problem solving?** *(Easy)(Skill 1.7)*

   A) guess and check
   B) look for key words to indicate operations such as all together—add, more than, subtract, times, multiply
   C) make a diagram
   D) solve a simpler version of the problem

The correct answer is B.
Answers A, C and D are all legitimate methods for approaching a problem. Answer B, on the other hand, is much less general and not as broadly applicable as the other answers, and therefore constitutes the least appropriate strategy.

8. **When you begin by assuming the conclusion of a theorem is false, then show that through a sequence of logically correct steps you contradict an accepted fact, this is known as** *(Easy)(Skill 1.8)*

   A) inductive reasoning
   B) direct proof
   C) indirect proof
   D) exhaustive proof

The correct answer is C.
By definition this describes the procedure of an indirect proof

9. The above diagram would be least appropriate for illustrating which of the following? *(Average)(Skill 2.1)*

A) $7 \times 4 + 3$
B) $31 \div 8$
C) 28×3
D) $31 - 3$

The correct answer is C.
C is inappropriate. A shows a 7x4 rectangle with 3 additional units. B is the division based on A. D shows how mental subtraction might be visualized leaving a composite difference.

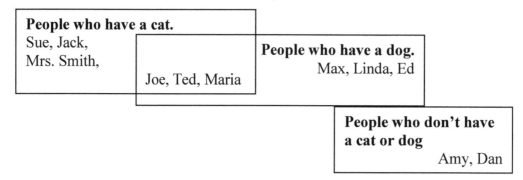

10. Which of the choices below does not represent a reasonable conclusion made from the Venn diagram? *(Average) (Skill 2.2)*

A) Amy has a fish
B) Mrs. Smith has a cat.
C) 3 people have a dog and a cat.
D) 6 people have a dog.

The correct answer is A.
No mention is made of any pet for Amy outside of the dog and cat she does not have. All other choices are true statements based on the diagram.

11. **Choose the least appropriate set of manipulatives for a sixth grade class. *(Easy)(Skill 2.3)***

    A) graphing calculators, compasses, rulers, conic section models
    B) two color counters, origami paper, markers, yarn
    C) balance, meter stick, colored pencils, beads
    D) paper cups, beans, tangrams, geoboards

The correct answer is A.
The manipulatives in answer A include tools that are most appropriate for students studying more advanced topics in algebra, such as functions and conic sections, as well as more advanced topics in geometry. As a result, these manipulatives may not be appropriate for sixth grade material. The other answers include manipulatives that may be more appropriate for a sixth grade class.

12. **Which of the following is not an example of Assistive Technology? *(Average) (Skill 2.4)***

    A) A worksheet that has been enlarged on a copy machine.
    B) A teacher microphone linked to a student speaker
    C) A closed circuit monitor displaying the teacher
    D) A set of place value blocks

The correct answer is D.
Choices A – C show how technology can be used to compensate for a student's handicap or physical challenge. Choice D is a manipulative that would actually present a challenge for someone with weak fine motor skills.

13. **A unit test covering three weeks of class material is best described as which kind of assessment? *(Easy) (Skill 3.1)***

    A) Final
    B) Formative
    C) Summative
    D) Directive

The correct answer is C.
Summative assessment is meant to measure the quality of learning over a specific period of time, while formative assessment helps monitor the process of learning.

14. Which of the following describe a technique that a teacher should use when analyzing student work and performance in order to improve student learning? *(Rigorous) (Skill 3.2)*

   A) Have a clear understanding of the student objectives
   B) Assess work according to set standards or rubrics
   C) Reflect on the overall class performance
   D) All of the above

The correct answer is D.
All of the above describe the way a student should look at student performance in order to ensure the analysis is fair and objective. Then appropriate steps can be taken to meet learning needs.

15. Which choice below shows the best example of how a teacher can use technology to efficiently analyze student performance? *(Average) (Skill 3.3)*

   A) Use an audience response system as part of the lesson.
   B) Have students raise their hands in response to a question.
   C) Tell students which numbers to type into their calculators.
   D) Have students type an equation into a graphing calculator.

The correct answer is A.
Choice A describes a way for a teacher to see a private, immediate response from each student. Furthermore, the response system can summarize trends in the received data to help a teacher see where to further adjust a lesson.

16. If a class performs poorly on a test, the teacher should *(Average) (Skill 3.4)*

   A) Make an easier test.
   B) Review results to see which items were most frequently missed and reteach those concepts.
   C) Not count the test toward the students' grades.
   D) Reteach the entire unit.

The correct answer is B.
Choice B describes a sound way to analyze student performance and adjust instruction as needed.

17. In order to question a student at a high level of cognitive complexity, *(Average) (Skill 3.5)*

   A) The teacher should ask questions about material that will be taught next year.
   B) The problem should use numbers with at least three digits.
   C) The question should integrate a need for processing skills and a series of multiple steps to reach the solution.
   D) The teacher should ask the question from the front of the room.

The correct answer is C.
An appropriate high level question should reflect the student's level of knowledge in a complex and multi-faceted way.

18. Higher order thinking, creativity, and the integration of reasoning and communication skills are most demonstrated by *(Easy) (Skill 3.6)*

   A) Multiple-choice and true/false tests
   B) Projects, demonstrations and oral presentations
   C) Essay questions
   D) Portfolios

The correct answer is B.
Projects, demonstrations and oral presentations call upon a variety of skills and allow for the greatest use of creativity and higher order thinking.
Alternative assessment is any type of assessment in which students express their understanding in a way other than just providing a question's answer.

19. When a math student returns from an absence, they should be encouraged to *(Easy) (Skill 4.1)*

   A) Not worry about the work that was missed
   B) Wait until the end of the chapter to complete any missed work
   C) Copy another student's homework
   D) Spend extra time completing any missed work as soon as possible.

The correct answer is D.
Since mathematics performance relies on the use of numerous prerequisite skills, a student needs to ensure all skills are understood in the appropriate order. If a student is lacking in a particular skill or understanding, he or she may not be able to progress through subsequent material.

TEACHER CERTIFICATION STUDY GUIDE

20. The phrase "two negatives make a positive" can cause a misconception when considering *(Average) (Skill 4.2)*

   A) The negative portions of the *x*- and *y*-axes on the coordinate plane
   B) The addition of two negative numbers versus the multiplication of two negative.
   C) Imaginary numbers
   D) none of the above

The correct answer is B.
The addition of two negative numbers leads to a negative answer, while multiplying two negative numbers has a positive result. Teachers should be certain to clarify the operation being considered.

21. Which of the following is not true about multiplication? *(Easy) (Skill 4.3)*

   A) Multiplication is only used in Algebra
   B) Multiplication represents repeated addition
   C) Multiplication is Commutative and Associative
   D) Multiplication can be modeled with area diagrams

The correct answer is A.
Multiplication is an operation naturally developing from (repeated) addition, and is used in all levels of Mathematics.

MIDDLE GRADES MATH. 5–9   203

22. A student turns in a paper with this type of error:

$7 + 16 \div 8 \times 2 = 8$

$8 - 3 \times 3 + 4 = -5$

(Rigorous)(Skill 4.4)

In order to remediate this error, a teacher should:

A) review and drill basic number facts

B) emphasize the importance of using parentheses in simplifying expressions

C) emphasize the importance of working from left to right when applying the order of operations

D) do nothing; these answers are correct

The correct answer is C.
In the above responses, the student has shown a tendency to perform operations out of the proper order. In the first case, the student has performed the multiplication and division in a right-to-left fashion, instead of left-to-right. As a result:

$$7 + 16 \div 8 \times 2 = 7 + 16 \div 16 = 7 + 1 = 8 \qquad 8 - 3 \times 3 + 4 = 8 - 9 + 4 = 8 - 13 = -5$$

These sequences are incorrect, but when a left-to-right approach is taken, the proper answers are determined.

$$7 + 16 \div 8 \times 2 = 7 + 2 \times 2 = 7 + 4 = 11 \qquad 8 - 3 \times 3 + 4 = 8 - 9 + 4 = -1 + 4 = 3$$

Thus, emphasizing the need to work from left to right for applying the order of operations would be the correct approach to dealing with the student's pattern of errors in this case.

23. Which of the following is a middle school mathematics skill that is needed for higher levels of math? *(Average) (Skill 4.5)*

   A) Number sense
   B) Recognizing patterns
   C) Knowing properties of Geometric shapes
   D) All of the above

The correct answer is D.
Choice A is necessary for further study of sets of numbers, like imaginary numbers. Choice B is the foundation of the study of Algebra. Choice C is essential for the study of Trigonometry.

24. Choose the set in which the members are not equivalent. *(Average)(Skill 5.1)*

   A) 1/2, 0.5, 50%
   B) 10/5, 2.0, 200%
   C) 3/8, 0.385, 38.5%
   D) 7/10, 0.7, 70%

The correct answer is C.
3/8 is equivalent to .375 and 37.5%.

25. When modeling the addition of the following numbers by hand: (-1) + 14 + 3 + 2 +18 +(-3) + 7, the teacher should *(Average) (Skill 5.2)*

   A) Round each value up
   B) Add all the negatives together first, then the positives
   C) First combine opposites, then add numbers that make sets of 10.
   D) Add the numbers up from left to right, then from right to left, and be sure the answers match.

The correct answer is C.
Choice C represents the most efficient way to find the total relying on the additive inverse property and the idea of clustering.

26. Which of the following is not true about the prime factorization of every composite number? *(Rigorous) (Skill 5.3)*

    A) The prime factorization will contain exponents
    B) The prime factorization can be used in simplifying expressions
    C) The prime factorization consists of prime numbers
    D) The prime factorization is unique.

The correct answer is A.
The prime factorization may or may not contain exponents. For instance: $35 = (5)(7)$ while $32 = 2^5$

27. Find the GCF of $2^2 \cdot 3^2 \cdot 5$ and $2^2 \cdot 3 \cdot 7$. *(Average)(Skill 5.4)*

    A) $2^5 \cdot 3^3 \cdot 5 \cdot 7$
    B) $2 \cdot 3 \cdot 5 \cdot 7$
    C) $2^2 \cdot 3$
    D) $2^3 \cdot 3^2 \cdot 5 \cdot 7$

The correct answer is C.
Choose the number of each prime factor that is in common.

28. If three cups of concentrate are needed to make 2 gallons of fruit punch, how many cups are needed to make 5 gallons? *(Easy)(Skill 5.5)*

    A) 6 cups
    B) 7 cups
    C) 7.5 cups
    D) 10 cups

The correct answer is C.
Set up the proportion $3/2 = x/5$, cross multiply to obtain $15=2x$, then divide both sides by 2.

29. Sandra has $34.00 and Carl has $42.00. Which would be the best method for determining how much more money Carl has than Sandra? *(Easy)(Skill 5.6)*

    A) addition
    B) subtraction
    C) division
    D) both A and B are equally correct

The correct answer is B.
To find how much more money Carl has than Sandra, it is necessary to subtract Sandra's amount from Carl's amount. This gives $42.00 - $34.00 = $8.00, which is indeed the difference. Answer B is the correct response.

30. {1,4,7,10, . . .} What is the 40th term in this sequence? *(Rigorous)(Skill 6.1)*

    A) 43
    B) 121
    C) 118
    D) 120

The correct answer is C.
The most direct way to determine the correct answer is to write out the entire sequence up to the 40th term. However, a much simpler method is more advisable. Consider that the 1st term is 1+0(3), the 2nd term is 1+1(3), the 3rd term is 1+2(3) and so on. Thus, following this pattern, the nth term of the sequence is 1+(n-1)3. Using this formula, it is sufficient to simply replace n with the number 40. This yields 1+(40-1)3 = 1+(39)3 = 1+117 = 118. Answer C is therefore correct.

31. Which set illustrates a function? *(Easy)(Skill 6.2)*

    A) { (0,1) (0,2) (0,3) (0,4) }
    B) { (3,9) (−3,9) (4,16) (− 4,16)}
    C) {(1,2) (2,3) (3,4) (1,4) }
    D) { (2,4) (3,6) (4,8) (4,16) }

The correct answer is B.
Each number in the domain can only be matched with one number in the range. A is not a function because 0 is mapped to 4 different numbers in the range. In C, 1 is mapped to two different numbers. In D, 4 is also mapped to two different numbers.

32. **Combine and simplify:** $\sqrt{75} + \sqrt{147} - \sqrt{48}$ *(Rigorous)(Skill 6.3)*

    A) 174

    B) $12\sqrt{3}$

    C) $8\sqrt{3}$

    D) 74

The correct answer is C.
Simplify each radical by factoring out the perfect squares:
$5\sqrt{3} + 7\sqrt{3} - 4\sqrt{3} = 8\sqrt{3}$

33. **Evaluate** $3^{1/2}(9^{1/3})$ *(Rigorous)(Skill 6.4)*

    A) $27^{5/6}$

    B) $9^{7/12}$

    C) $3^{5/6}$

    D) $3^{6/7}$

The correct answer is B.
Getting the bases the same gives us $3^{\frac{1}{2}}3^{\frac{2}{3}}$. Adding exponents gives $3^{\frac{7}{6}}$. Then some additional manipulation of exponents produces $3^{\frac{7}{6}} = 3^{\frac{14}{12}} = \left(3^2\right)^{\frac{7}{12}} = 9^{\frac{7}{12}}$.

34. **Solve for** *x*: **3x + 5 ≥ 8 + 7x** *(Average)(Skill 6.5)*

    A) $x \geq -\dfrac{3}{4}$

    B) $x \leq -\dfrac{3}{4}$

    C) $x \geq \dfrac{3}{4}$

    D) $x \leq \dfrac{3}{4}$

The correct answer is B.
Using additive equality, $-3 \geq 4x$. Divide both sides by 4 to obtain $-3/4 \geq x$. Carefully determine which answer choice is equivalent.

35. Solve for x: $|2x+3| > 4$ *(Rigorous)(Skill 6.5)*

A) $-\frac{7}{2} > x > \frac{1}{2}$

B) $-\frac{1}{2} > x > \frac{7}{2}$

C) $x < \frac{7}{2}$ or $x < -\frac{1}{2}$

D) $x < -\frac{7}{2}$ or $x > \frac{1}{2}$

The correct answer is D.
The quantity within the absolute value symbols must be either > 4 or < -4.
Solve the two inequalities $2x + 3 > 4$ or $2x + 3 < -4$

36. Which graph represents the solution set for $x^2 + 6 > 5x$?
(Rigorous) (Skill 6.6)

A)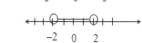
   -2 0   2

B)
   -3   0   3

C)
   -2   0   2 |

D)
   -3   0   2 3

The correct answer is D.
Rewriting the inequality gives $x^2 - 5x + 6 > 0$. Factoring gives $(x - 2)(x - 3) > 0$.
The two cut-off points on the number line are now at $x = 2$ and $x = 3$. Choosing a random number in each of the three parts of the number line, we test them to see if they produce a true statement. If $x = 0$ or $x = 4$, $(x-2)(x-3)>0$ is true. If $x = 2.5$, $(x-2)(x-3)>0$ is false. Therefore, the solution set is all numbers smaller than 2 or greater than 3.

37. Identify the proper sequencing of subskills when teaching graphing inequalities in two dimensions *(Easy)(Skill 6.7)*

   A) shading regions, graphing lines, graphing points, determining whether a line is solid or broken
   B) graphing points, graphing lines, determining whether a line is solid or broken, shading regions
   C) graphing points, shading regions, determining whether a line is solid or broken, graphing lines
   D) graphing lines, determining whether a line is solid or broken, graphing points, shading regions

The correct answer is B.
Graphing points is the most fundamental subskill for graphing inequalities in two dimensions. Next follows the graphing of lines, and then determining whether the line is solid or broken. The graphing of lines requires, at a minimum, the graphing of two points (such as the *x*- and *y*-intercepts). Once the line has been graphed (perhaps with a light marking), it can next be determined whether the line is solid or broken, depending on the inequality being graphed. Finally, the shading of appropriate regions on the graph may be undertaken.

38. A burning candle loses ½ inch in height every hour. If the original height of the candle was 6 inches, which of the following equations describes the relationship between the height h of the candle and the number of hours t since it was lit? *(Rigorous)(Skill 6.8)*

   A) $2h + t = 12$
   B) $2h - t = 12$
   C) $h = 6 - t$
   D) $h = 0.5t + 6$

The correct answer is A.
Since the height of the candle is falling, the slope = -1/2. Thus, the equation in the slope-intercept form is $h = -(1/2)t + 6$ since h = 6 for t = 0. Multiplying both sides of the equation by 2, we get $2h = -t + 12$ or $2h + t = 12$.

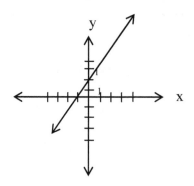

39. What is the equation of the above graph? *(Rigorous)(Skill 6.9)*

    A) $2x + y = 2$
    B) $2x - y = -2$
    C) $2x - y = 2$
    D) $2x + y = -2$

The correct answer is B.
By observation, we see that the graph has a y-intercept of 2 and a slope of 2/1 = 2. Therefore its equation is $y = mx + b = 2x + 2$. Rearranging the terms gives $2x - y = -2$.

40. Put the following numbers in order from least to greatest. *(Average)(Skill 6.10)*

    12.2, 0, 7, $\sqrt{14}$, $\sqrt{25}$, $\sqrt{\frac{1}{4}}$, 3 x 10⁻⁴

    A) 12.2, 0, 7, $\sqrt{14}$, $\sqrt{25}$, $\sqrt{\frac{1}{4}}$, 3 x 10⁻⁴

    B) 3 x 10⁻⁴, 0, 7, 12.2, $\sqrt{14}$, $\sqrt{25}$, $\sqrt{\frac{1}{4}}$

    C) 0, $\sqrt{\frac{1}{4}}$, 7, 12.2, $\sqrt{14}$, $\sqrt{25}$, 3 x 10⁻⁴

    D) 0, 3 x 10⁻⁴, $\sqrt{\frac{1}{4}}$, $\sqrt{14}$, $\sqrt{25}$, 7, 12.2

The correct answer is D.
The value 3 x 10⁻⁴ is equivalent to .0003 which is a positive number smaller than .5, the equivalent of $\sqrt{\frac{1}{4}}$. An estimate of $\sqrt{14}$ puts its value between 3, $\sqrt{9}$, and 4, $\sqrt{16}$. The largest values in the list are 7 and 12.2.

41. **Which statement is an example of the additive identity?**
    (Easy)(Skill 6.11)

    A) $3 + -3 = 0$
    B) $3x = 3x + 0$
    C) $3 \cdot \dfrac{1}{3} = 1$
    D) $3 + 2x = 2x + 3$

The correct answer is B.
B Illustrates the identity property of addition. A illustrates additive inverse, C illustrates the multiplicative inverse, and D illustrates the commutative property of addition.

42. **Given a graph for a function $f(x)$ describe how the graph of $-f(x)$ will compare to the original.** *(Easy) (Skill 7.1)*

    A) Flipped over the x- axis
    B) Flipped over the y- axis
    C) Rotated 90°
    D) Unchanged

The correct answer is A.
Changing $f(x)$ to $-f(x)$ will make every y value the opposite of what it was originally, thereby turning the graph upside down, or flipping it over the x- axis.

43. **What is the slope of any line parallel to the line 2x + 4y = 4?**
    (Rigorous)(Skill 7.2)

    A) -2
    B) -1
    C) – ½
    D) 2

The correct answer is C.
The formula for slope is $y = mx + b$, where m is the slope. Lines that are parallel have the same slope.

$$2x + 4y = 4$$
$$4y = -2x + 4$$
$$y = \frac{-2x}{4} + 1$$
$$y = \frac{-1}{2}x + 1$$

44. Factor completely: $8(x - y) + a(y - x)$ *(Rigorous)(Skill 7.3)*

    A) $(8 + a)(y - x)$
    B) $(8 - a)(y - x)$
    C) $(a - 8)(y - x)$
    D) $(a - 8)(y + x)$

The correct answer is C.
Glancing first at the solution choices, factor $(y - x)$ from each term. This leaves -8 from the first term and a from the second term: $(a - 8)(y - x)$

45. Find the zeroes of $f(x) = x^3 + x^2 - 14x - 24$ *(Rigorous)(Skill 7.3)*

    A) $4,\ 3,\ 2$
    B) $3,\ -8$
    C) $7,\ -2,\ -1$
    D) $4,\ -3,\ -2$

The correct answer is D.
Possible rational roots of the equation $0 = x^3 + x^2 - 14x - 24$ are all the positive and negative factors of 24. By substituting into the equation, we find that -2 is a root, and therefore that $x+2$ is a factor. By performing the long division $(x^3 + x^2 - 14x - 24)/(x+2)$, we can find that another factor of the original equation is $x^2 - x - 12$ or $(x-4)(x+3)$. Therefore the zeros of the original function are -2, -3, and 4.

46. Solve for x and y: $x = 3y + 7$, $7x + 5y = 23$ *(Rigorous)(Skill 7.4)*

    A) $(-1,4)$
    B) $(4, -1)$
    C) $(\frac{-29}{7}, \frac{-26}{7})$
    D) $(10, 1)$

The correct answer is B.
Substituting x in the second equation results in $7(3y + 7) + 5y = 23$. Solve by distributing and grouping like terms: $26y+49 = 23$, $26y = -26$, $y = -1$.
Substitute y into the first equation to obtain x. $x = 3(-1) + 7 = -3 + 7 = 4$

47. Which graph shows the solution to the system of inequalities below?

$3x - 2y \leq 5$

$-x + 5y > 1$

(Rigorous) (Skill 7.5)

A)

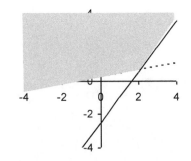

B)

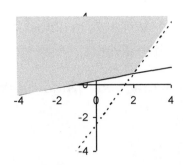

C)

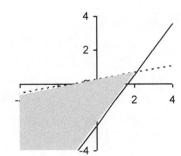

D)

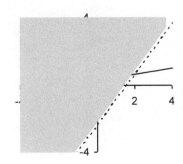

The correct answer is A.
First, solve each inequality for y, as shown below.

$3x - 2y \leq 5$	$-x + 5y > 1$
$2y + 5 \geq 3x$	$5y > x + 1$
$2y \geq 3x - 5$	$y > 0.2x + 0.2$
$y \geq 1.5x - 2.5$	

These two linear inequalities can be plotted separately on the same graph. Recall that the boundary line of the solution set is found by replacing the inequality symbol ($\geq$ or $>$, in this case) with an equality. If the inequality is absolute ($>$ or $<$), a dashed line is used, since the points on the line do not satisfy the inequality. Otherwise, a solid line is used. The appropriate region can then be shaded.

48. Solve for x. $3x^2 - 2 + 4(x^2 - 3) = 0$ *(Rigorous)(Skill 7.6)*

A) $\{ -\sqrt{2} , \sqrt{2} \}$
B) $\{ 2, -2 \}$
C) $\{ 0, \sqrt{3}, -\sqrt{3} \}$
D) $\{ 7, -7 \}$

The correct answer is A.
Distribute and combine like terms to obtain $7x^2 - 14 = 0$.
Add 14 to both sides, then divide by 7. Since $x^2 = 2$, $x = \pm\sqrt{2}$

49. Which equation is graphed? *(Rigorous)(Skill 7.7)*

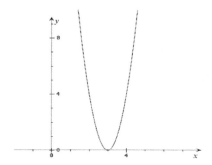

A) $y = 4 (x + 3)^2$
B) $y = 4 (x - 3)^2$
C) $y = 3 (x - 4)^2$
D) $y = 3 (x + 4)^2$

The correct answer is B.
Since the vertex of the parabola is three units to the left, we choose the solution where 3 is subtracted from x, then the quantity is squared. Another way to look at this is to check the point (3,0), visible on the graph, in each equation. Only choice B works.

50. Solve for x: $\sqrt{3 - 2x} = 7$ *(Average) (Skill 7.8)*

A) -23
B) -2
C) 5
D) no solution

The correct answer is A.
To solve a radical equation, square both sides: $3 - 2x = 49$,
then solve for x. $-2x = 46$, $x = -23$.

Check the answer: $\sqrt{3 - 2(-23)} = \sqrt{3 + 46} = \sqrt{49} = 7$

51. 2^{-3} is equivalent to *(Average)(Skill 7.9)*

A) 0.8
B) −0.8
C) 125
D) 0.125

The correct answer is D.
Express as the fraction 1/8, then convert to a decimal. $2^{-3} = \frac{1}{2^3} = \frac{1}{8} \to 0.125$

52. Which of the following is incorrect? *(Rigorous)(Skill 7.9)*

A) $(x^2 y^3)^2 = x^4 y^6$
B) $m^2 (2n)^3 = 8m^2 n^3$
C) $(m^3 n^4)/(m^2 n^2) = mn^2$
D) $(x + y^2)^2 = x^2 + y^4$

The correct answer is D.
Using FOIL to do the expansion: $(x + y^2)^2 = (x + y^2)(x + y^2) = x^2 + 2xy^2 + y^4$.

53. Compute the median for the following data set: {12, 19, 13, 16, 17, 14} *(Average)(Skill 8.1)*

A) 14.5
B) 15.17
C) 15
D) 16

The correct answer is C.
Arrange the data in ascending order: 12,13,14,16,17,19. The median is the middle value in a list with an odd number of entries. When there is an even number of entries, the median is the mean of the two center entries. Here the average of 14 and 16 is 15.

54. Corporate salaries are listed for several employees. Which best describes the range of the data? *(Average)(Skill 8.2)*

$24,000 $24,000 $26,000 $28,000 $30,000 $120,000

A) $96,000
B.) $120,000
C) $120,000 - $24,000
D) no range

The correct answer is A.
The range is the difference between the largest and smallest value in a set of data.

55. What conclusion can be drawn from the graph below? *(Average)(Skill 8.3)*

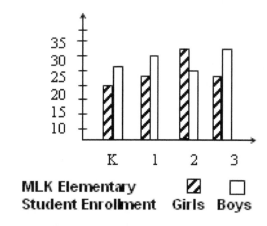

MLK Elementary
Student Enrollment   Girls Boys

A) The number of students in first grade exceeds the number in second grade.
B) There are more boys than girls in the entire school.
C) There are more girls than boys in the first grade.
D) Third grade has the largest number of students.

The correct answer is B.
In Kindergarten, first grade, and third grade, there are more boys than girls. The number of extra girls in grade two is more than made up for by the extra boys in all the other grades put together.

56. **Which of the following types of graphs would be best to use to record the eye color of the students in the class? (Average) (Skill 8.4)**

   A) Bar graph or circle graph
   B) Pictograph or bar graph
   C) Line graph or pictograph
   D) Line graph or bar graph

The correct answer is B.
A pictograph or a bar graph could be used. In this activity, a line graph would not be used because it shows change over time. Although a circle graph could be used to show a percentage of students with brown eyes, blue eyes, etc. that representation would be too advanced for early childhood students.

57. **How many ways are there to choose a potato and two green vegetables from a choice of three potatoes and seven green vegetables? (Rigorous)(Skill 8.5)**

   A) 126
   B) 63
   C) 21
   D) 252

The correct answer is B.
There are $\binom{3}{1} = \frac{3!}{1!(2-1)!} = 3$ ways to choose the potato, and there are
$\binom{7}{2} = \frac{7!}{2!(7-2)!} = 21$ ways to choose the green vegetable. So there are $3 \cdot 21 = 63$
ways to choose a potato and a green vegetable.

58. **A sack of candy has 3 peppermints, 2 butterscotch drops and 3 cinnamon drops. One candy is drawn and replaced, then another candy is drawn; what is the probability that both will be butterscotch? (Average)(Skill 8.6)**

   A) 1/2
   B) 1/28
   C) 1/4
   D) 1/16

The correct answer is D.
With replacement, the probability of obtaining a butterscotch on the first draw is 2/8 and the probability of drawing a butterscotch on the second draw is also 2/8. Multiply and reduce to lowest terms.

59. Which of the following is a correct name for the ray? *(Easy) (Skill 9.1)*

A) $\overrightarrow{PU}$
B) $\overrightarrow{PT}$
C) $\overrightarrow{UT}$
D) Both A and B

The correct answer is D.
A ray must be named with two points: the endpoint is listed first, followed by any other point on the ray.

60. Given $l_1 \parallel l_2$ which of the following is true? *(Average)(Skill 9.2)*

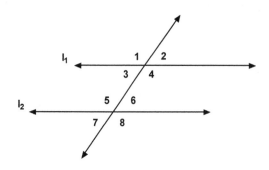

A) $\angle 1$ and $\angle 8$ are congruent and alternate interior angles
B) $\angle 2$ and $\angle 3$ are congruent and corresponding angles
C) $\angle 3$ and $\angle 4$ are adjacent and supplementary angles
D) $\angle 3$ and $\angle 5$ are adjacent and supplementary angles

The correct answer is C.
The angles in A are exterior. In B, the angles are vertical. The angles in D are consecutive, not adjacent.

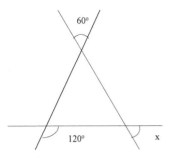

Note: Figure not drawn to scale.

61. In the figure above, what is the value of x? *(Rigorous)(Skill 9.8)*

A) 50°
B) 60°
C) 75°
D) 80°

The correct answer is B.
The angles within the triangle make up 180°. Opposite angles are equal, therefore, the angle opposite the 60° angle is also 60°. Adjacent angles add to 180° (straight line). Therefore, the angle inside the triangle adjacent to the 120° angle is 60°. The third angle in the triangle would then be 60° (180° – 60° – 60°). Since x is opposite this third angle, it would also be 60°.

62. What is the degree measure of an interior angle of a regular 10-sided polygon? *(Rigorous)(Skill 9.3)*

A) 18°
B) 36°
C) 144°
D) 54°

The correct answer is C.
Formula for finding the measure of each interior angle of a regular polygon with n sides is $\dfrac{(n-2)180°}{n}$.

For n=10, we get $\dfrac{8(180°)}{10} = 144°$.

63. Given ΔDOG is isosceles with $\overline{DO} \cong \overline{OG}$ and m<O = 22°, find m<D. (Easy)(Skill 9.4)

   A) 180°
   B) 158°
   C) 79°
   D) none of the above

The correct answer is C.
Since $\overline{DO}$ and $\overline{OG}$ are the congruent legs of the triangle, the congruent base angles are <D and <G. Let the measure of a base angle = x.
180° = 2x + 22°, x = 79°

64. Given any ΔABC, which of the following statements might not be true? (Rigorous)(Skill 9.5)

   A) m<A + m<B + m<C = 180°
   B) a + b >c
   C) b + c >a
   D) $a^2 + b^2 = c^2$

The correct answer is D.
Choice A is true for angles that make up any triangle. Choices B and C are true for sides of every triangle. But choice D is only true for right triangles, and ΔABC was not given as a right triangle.

65. Which theorem can be used to prove $\triangle BAK \cong \triangle MKA$? (Rigorous)(Skill 9.6)

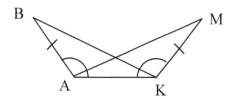

   A) SSS
   B) ASA
   C) SAS
   D) AAS

The correct answer is C.
Since side AK is common to both triangles, the triangles can be proven congruent by using the Side-Angle-Side Postulate.

66. Ginny and Nick head back to their respective colleges after being home for the weekend. They leave their house at the same time and drive for 4 hours. Ginny drives due south at the average rate of 60 miles per hour and Nick drives due east at the average rate of 60 miles per hour. What is the straight-line distance between them, in miles, at the end of the 4 hours? *(Rigorous)(Skill 9.7)*

A) $120\sqrt{2}$
B) 240
C) $240\sqrt{2}$
D) 288

The correct answer is C.
Draw a picture.

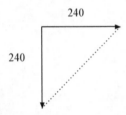

We have a right triangle, so we can use the Pythagorean Theorem to find the distance between the two points.

$$240^2 + 240^2 = c^2$$
$$2(240)^2 = c^2$$
$$240\sqrt{2} = c$$

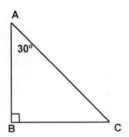

67. If AC = 12, determine BC. *(Average)(Skill 9.7)*

    A) 6
    B) 4
    C) $6\sqrt{3}$
    D) $3\sqrt{6}$

The correct answer is A.
In a 30-60-90 right triangle, the leg opposite the 30° angle is half the length of the hypotenuse.

68. Determine the measures of angles A and B. *(Average) (Skill 9.8)*

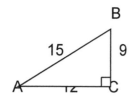

    A) A = 30°, B = 60°
    B) A = 60°, B = 30°
    C) A = 53°, B = 37°
    D) A = 37°, B = 53°

The correct answer is D.
tan A = 9/12=.75 and tan⁻¹.75 = 37° . Since angle B is complementary to angle A, the measure of angle B is therefore 53° .

69. Which of the following is true about a parallelogram?
(Average)(Skill 9.9)

    A) The opposite sides are congruent.
    B) The diagonals are congruent.
    C) All four angles are congruent.
    D) The sum of the interior angles is 180°.

The correct answer is A.
Choices B and C are true for rectangles. Choice D is true for triangles

70. Given segment AC with B as its midpoint find the coordinates of C if
    A = (5, 7) and B = (3, 6.5). *(Rigorous)(Skill 9.10)*

   A) (4, 6.5)
   B) (1, 6)
   C) (2, 0.5)
   D) (16, 1)

The correct answer is B.
The formula for the midpoint of a segment with endpoints (x_1, y_1) and (x_2, y_2) is:

$$\left(x_{mid}, y_{mid}\right) = \left(\frac{x_1 + x_2}{2}, \frac{y_1 + y_2}{2}\right)$$

Expressing this formula in terms of the given information (coordinates of points A and B) yields:

$$\left(3, 6.5\right) = \left(\frac{5 + x_C}{2}, \frac{7 + y_C}{2}\right)$$

Each coordinate may be found by algebraically solving the two resulting equations:

$$3 = \frac{5 + x_C}{2} \qquad\qquad 6.5 = \frac{7 + y_C}{2}$$

$$6 = 5 + x_C \qquad\qquad 13 = 7 + y_C$$

$$x_C = 1 \qquad\qquad y_C = 6$$

Thus, the correct answer is (1, 6).

71. Find the distance between (3, 7) and (−3, 4). *(Average)(Skill 9.10)*

    A) 9
    B) 45
    C) $3\sqrt{5}$
    D) $5\sqrt{3}$

The correct answer is C.
Using the distance formula

$$\sqrt{(4-7)^2+(-3-3)^2}=\sqrt{(-3)^2+(-6)^2}=\sqrt{9+36}=\sqrt{45}=3\sqrt{5}$$

72. In similar polygons, if the perimeters are in a ratio of x : y, the sides are in a ratio of *(Rigorous)(Skill 9.11)*

    A) x : y
    B) $x^2 : y^2$
    C) 2x : y
    D) 1/2 x : y

The correct answer is A.
In similar polygons, the sides and perimeters are in the same ratio.

73. If a circle has an area of 25 cm², what is its circumference, to the nearest tenth of a centimeter? *(Rigorous)(Skill 9.12)*

    A) 78.5 cm
    B) 17.7 cm
    C) 8.9 cm
    D) 15.7 cm

The correct answer is B.
Find the radius by solving $A = \pi r^2$. 25$= \pi r^2$; r =2.82. Then substitute r=2.82 into $C = 2\pi r$ to obtain the circumference. $C = 2\pi \cdot 2.82 = 17.7$

74. 4 square yards is equivalent to *(Average)(Skill 10.1)*

   A) 12 square feet
   B) 48 square feet
   C) 36 square feet
   D) 108 square feet

The correct answer is C.
There are 9 square feet in a square yard, so 4(9) = 36.

$$4yd^2 \cdot \frac{9ft^2}{1yd^2} = 36ft^2$$

75. Find the area of the figure below. *(Rigorous)(Skill 10.2)*

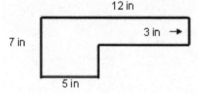

   A) 56 in²
   B) 27 in²
   C) 71 in²
   D) 170 in²

The correct answer is A.
Divide the figure into two rectangles with a horizontal line. The area of the top rectangle is 36 in, and the bottom is 20 in.

76. Determine the volume of a sphere to the nearest cm if the surface area is 113 cm². *(Rigorous)(Skill 10.2)*

   A) 113 cm³
   B) 339 cm³
   C) 37.7 cm³
   D) 226 cm3

The correct answer is A.
Solve for the radius of the sphere using $A = 4\pi r^2$. The radius is 3. Then, find the volume using $V = \frac{4}{3}\pi r^3$. Note: Only when the radius is 3 are the volume and surface area equivalent.

77. If the radius of a right circular cylinder is doubled, how does its volume change? *(Rigorous)(Skills 10.3)*

 A) no change
 B) also is doubled
 C) four times the original
 D) pi times the original

The correct answer is C.
If the radius of a right circular cylinder is doubled, the volume is multiplied by four because in the formula ($V = \pi r^2 h$), the radius is squared. Therefore, the new volume is 2^2 or four times the original.

78. A figure with 6 faces can be *(Easy)(Skill 10.4)*

 A) a hexagon
 B) a cylinder
 C) a sphere
 D) a cube

The correct answer is D.
While a hexagon does have 6 sides, it does not have 6 faces. Faces imply a three-dimensional figure. A cube does have 6 faces. A cylinder and sphere do not have faces due to their circular nature.

79. Giving students a worksheet with a pattern to color, cut out, and fold into a tetrahedron would be *(Rigorous) (Skill 10.5)*

 A) A way for students to work with the net of a three-dimensional figure
 B) An opportunity for students to learn how to share craft supplies.
 C) A proof of congruent triangles.
 D) An example of the Commutative Property of Addition.

The correct answer is A.
The process explained fits the description of taking the net of a 3-D figure and turning it into a model.

80. Which of the following techniques or features can be used when drawing a 3-D figure on a piece of paper? *(Average Rigor)(Skill 10.6)*

   A) shading
   B) dotted lines
   C) a set of 3-D coordinate axes
   D) all of the above

The correct answer is D.
All of the choices are good ways to make an object appear three-dimensional despite its representation on a two-dimensional piece of paper.

CPSIA information can be obtained
at www.ICGtesting.com
Printed in the USA
BVHW011125010219
539256BV00014B/286/P